HOW TO CREATE HISTORY

AN AUTHOR'S GUIDE TO CREATING HISTORY, MYTHS, AND MONSTERS

A TREVENA

ISBN: 9781838327330

Cover design by P&V Digital

Published by Maythorne Press
www.maythornepress.co.uk

How to Create History is also available as an ebook Guidebook.

The content of the ebook is the same. It offers a more portable version of this workbook, and simply requires you to provide your own space for notes.

AUTHOR GUIDES SERIES

30 DAYS OF WORLDBUILDING
An Author's Step-by-Step Guide to Building Fictional Worlds

HOW TO DESTROY THE WORLD
An Author's Guide to Writing Dystopia and Post-Apocalypse

FROM SANCTITY TO SORCERY
An Author's Guide to Building Belief Structures and Magic Systems

HOW TO CREATE HISTORY
An Author's Guide to Creating History, Myths, and Monsters

COMPLETE WORLDBUILDING
An Author's Step-by-Step Guide to Building Fictional Worlds

angelinetrevena.co.uk/worldbuilding

CONTENTS

INTRODUCTION

I am one of those authors who have been writing, pretty much, since they were old enough to hold a pen. I have a folder of old stories, typed up on an old typewriter, that I don't even remember having written.

I was rarely seen without a book in my hand, and spent every spare hour I had, buried deep in fantastical worlds. I was lucky in that my parents encouraged it. They never told me that I was wasting my time, or to keep my head out of the clouds. They even let me read at the dinner table, eating one-handed.

I was also lucky to have access to a local library, and quickly worked my way through the fantasy catalogue in their children's section. I swept my way through all of the Choose Your Own Adventure books; not only following the adventures of kids—passing into a fantasy world to fight dragons, mounted on their bicycle steeds—but I got to control the stories. I could re-read them over and over, choosing different paths each time, creating a multitude of adventures for myself.

My love of speculative fiction had started young. It was my dad's job to read the bedtime stories each night, all of us huddled together to listen. He often picked books from his own collection which, almost exclusively, consisted of classic sci-fi novels. And so, as a child, my bedtime stories were written by the likes of H.G. Wells and John Wyndham. Looking back, I suspect that *The War of the Worlds* and *The Day of the Triffids* were probably inappropriate choices for children about to go to sleep, but it must have caught my imagination. I will forever thank my dad for introducing me to such tales.

At the age of 16 I finally picked up the Chronicles of Narnia books, reading all seven of them in just five days. It was then that my Narnia obsession began, and it has never waned.

Before starting at university, I worked in an antique auction house. Every wardrobe that came through the saleroom, I would check in the back of it for Narnia. It reached the point that the staff would come and inform me each time they took receipt of one!

When they announced the latest film adaptations, I scoured the internet daily for news. I saw each of them on their day of release, going to the cinema alone for an uninterrupted experience. A pure absorption of them. I can still name the four actors who portrayed the Pevensie children, their names branded into my memory. Yes, the woman who can't even remember her own phone number!

One of my most treasured possessions is an old wardrobe. I bought it from a second-hand furniture shop for just £20. It has moved house with us several times, and has practically fallen apart, with my husband tasked with fixing it back together. Carved into its door is a beautiful rendering of a ship, in full sail, riding the sea. And the serpentine hinges on it are like sea monsters. It is beautiful, and largely useless. It isn't deep enough to hold a standard coat hanger on its rail, and the mirror on the back of the door is so mottled and degraded it hardly reflects anything at all. In fact, it has rarely ever been used as an actual wardrobe, and currently holds my increasingly out of control to-be-read pile.

But, because it looks like it may have once stood in the captain's quarters on board the Dawntreader, I will never part with it.

And, over the years, I have collected other bits and pieces that remind me of Narnia. Including film props, and a good collection of behind-the-scenes and the-making-of books. My obsession is complete, and incurable. All that is left is to find a way to Narnia myself. I'm still looking, and I won't give up.

Despite this, I did stray from my love of fantasy. At university I studied Drama and Creative Writing, and wandered away from magic and fantastical worlds. I can't say why, it just happened. Perhaps I felt pressure to finally grow up. Perhaps my university course pushed me towards literary fiction. Perhaps I simply needed a break from it for a while. I don't know.

After university, as I began to navigate the confusing and cynical world of adulthood, I barely read anything at all. For a long time, I hardly managed a handful of books a year. During this time, I read my first ever Stephen King book. It was, interestingly enough, *On Writing* that I picked up first, and I finished it in just a few days. And so, I was brought back to literature with a renewed desire to read, as well as to write.

Although I've been writing since I was very young, it was never my ambition to make a career from it. I wanted to act. I wanted to be on stage. My whole childhood was filled with drama lessons, singing lessons, lessons in several different forms of dance. I was always performing; music concerts, amateur dramatics, school plays. If there was a spotlight, I was in it.

While I was at university, studying Drama, I discovered that I wasn't enjoying it as much as I'd expected to. I had a long heart-to-heart with myself, finally accepting that the ambition I'd had all of my life, my singular goal, simply wasn't what I wanted anymore. And it was difficult to let go of. This vision had shaped my entire life, my entire personality, and I had nothing to replace it with.

But, I couldn't pretend to myself anymore. And, as I continued with my degree, I came to the conclusion that I didn't want to be onstage, blinking into the spotlight, speaking someone else's words. What I wanted was to sit in the back of a darkened auditorium, watching other people perform my words. I wanted to write.

Even with this revelation, I still didn't imagine myself making writing into any kind of a career. The first Kindle wouldn't come on the market for another six years. The publishing landscape was a very different one to what it is today. Becoming a published author was a pipe-dream. One that seemed to rely far more on luck than any kind of talent. A who-you-know rather than a what-you-know industry. And for a young woman barely into her twenties, and still reeling from losing the footing of the one constant she'd had in her life, it all seemed like an impossibility.

As part of my Creative Writing class, our tutor asked us to write a personal introduction to an imaginary book about ourselves. Much like this introduction you're reading right now. The difference being, in that imagined introduction, I wrote "I can't imagine writing ever being anything more than a hobby for me." When I wrote that, I wouldn't have believed I'd ever be writing one for real.

When our assignments were returned, my tutor had highlighted that sentence, responding with the note "That would be a shame." That single comment began a shift in mindset which, over the following years, led me to this moment right now. And this book, through all those that have come before it.

Inspiration tends to come from the most unexpected sources, at the most unexpected of moments.

And I'm sure that my tutor has no idea of the impact she had. Of the wheels she set into motion. Of the future she helped to craft. She dropped a small pebble into a pool, and its ripples are still radiating outwards.

USING THIS WORKBOOK

If you're looking to deepen the history of your world, and you're not sure where to start, this is the book for you. If you'd like to create ancient myths and legends, this is the book for you. If you find the idea of constructing histories daunting, and you've been putting off starting to build your world, this is definitely the book for you.

This workbook breaks down the task of creating histories, showing you how to pick out the important moments and events. It will lead you through the process of tying your world's history to the timeline, story, and characters in your book. It will explain how you can use myths and legends to explore themes and cause conflict. And it will show you that monsters can do so much more than simply scare your readers.

This book and its prompts are not, by any means, exhaustive. Depending on your genre, your story, your characters, and the world you need to create for them, you may need aspects that are not covered by this workbook. Likewise, some of these prompts may not be relevant to you.

Think of it like a garden. This book gives you the foundation to build upon. It helps you to plant the seeds, and offers you seeds you may not have considered planting yourself. But, you'll need to cultivate it, and water it. And, you may have plants of your own that you want to include. A special tree, your favourite flower. You may like to have a pond, or a bench, or a marquee.

The other thing this workbook offers is a safe, singular place to keep all of your worldbuilding notes. It's surprisingly easy to get lost in your own world, and surprisingly easy to forget the details of it. This will become your worldbuilding bible. Your one-stop-shop for everything you need to know about your world. When you come to writing your story, keep this book next to you, so that everything you need to know about your world is in easy reach.

I have purposefully left the work pages of this book as blank as possible, because we all like to work in different ways. Draw pictures, create tables and graphs, or fill it with neatly written notes. Use it in the way that works best for you.

Above all, enjoy your worldbuilding. Enjoy exploring it, and watching it come to life around you.

As a simple human, this may be the closest you'll come to performing real magic. To visualise an entire world from nothing. To pluck things from the air and make them real. To take breath on the wind and form it into something tangible. That is the most real, purest magic I know of.

Of course, I'm being presumptuous here. You may have magical abilities beyond my comprehension. In fact, you may even be a little more than human...

WORLDBUILDING BASICS

While fantasy and science-fiction authors may be doing the heavy lifting when creating their fictional worlds, worldbuilding exists in, pretty much, every genre. To a certain extent.

Whether it's the creation of an imaginary cafe in a real town, or imagining an alternative outcome to an event from history, any book, of any kind, can involve worldbuilding. At the fantasy, sci-fi, and horror end of the scale, the worldbuilding-heavyweights, it may mean the creation of a magic system, or monsters, to slot alongside the real world. Or it may mean building an entirely new world with new species and cultures, right up to an entire universe of planets.

It can become quite the epic task!

Now, I don't know about you, but I tend to get easily overwhelmed by epic tasks. That's why I'm still working up to de-cluttering my house. I just look at the job as a whole, can't untangle where to actually start, and I end up doing nothing at all.

As much as I understand the usefulness and the importance of breaking things down into workable chunks, into simple steps, the ability and method for doing this very often escapes me. Unlike many other people, I can see the wood very clearly. It's the trees I have trouble with.

Worldbuilding doesn't need to be difficult, or complicated. It doesn't need to take forever, or be an excuse for never actually writing the book. It doesn't need to be overwhelming or intimidating. At the other end of the scale, it shouldn't be something that you haphazardly bolt on in a last-minute panic.

As you'll discover through this book, worldbuilding should be tightly integrated with your plot and your characters. Your characters, and their goals, their struggles, their journey, that is the reason your readers show up. That's the reason they keep reading. You can have the most amazing world, but if you don't populate it with compelling, sympathetic, and relatable characters, readers will simply stop turning the pages. Likewise, if you write amazing characters, and put them into a flat, paper world, your readers won't want to walk along with them, or explore with them.

Just as you want your readers to believe in your characters, you want them to believe in your world, too.

Let them smell the salt on the breeze, hear the buzzing of the insects. Let them feel the heat of the burning buildings, and feel the oppression of the government. Let them walk every single step with your characters. Invite them in. And invite them to stay. Whether they want to set up home there, or fight to change it.

Your worldbuilding is equally as important as your story and characters. Give your characters somewhere real to live, and give your readers somewhere real to visit. You simply can't separate these things out if you want to write the best book that you can.

So, what are you waiting for? Let's get started with the basics of worldbuilding.

DIFFERENT TYPES OF WORLDBUILDING

There are a few different ways to approach worldbuilding, and which you choose, will depend on your goals, your story, and your genre.

Building a whole new fictional world:
This is mostly used for writing fantasy and science fiction, and involves creating an entirely fictional world from scratch. Somewhere that does not, and never has, existed. It may have similarities to our world, and it may have huge differences. Think along the lines of second-world fantasies penned by the likes of J.R.R. Tolkien or C.S. Lewis.

A real place with an alternative past or future:
This may be taking a real existing place, London, for example, and giving it an alternative or altered history. Imagine if the Great Fire of London had actually been started by dragons. How would that change the world today? Or it may be taking the real-world place, and throwing it into your imagined future. This is very common in dystopia, imagining an unpleasant future for our world.

When using this style of worldbuilding, your map is usually, largely, already done for you. There is likely to be some changes, such as missing landmarks, or different names for places. The extent of the changes would entirely depend on your story, and how different you have imagined the past or future of this place.

A real place with a parallel fictional world:
The other way is to set your story in a real place, and have a fictional world created alongside it, usually invisible or hidden from the general public. Such as in Neil Gaiman's Neverwhere, or Harry Potter, or Hellboy. The fictional side of the world may be tightly integrated with the real world, or it may be quite separate. This would depend, again, on your story.

Whichever kind of world you're building, your objective is still the same: to create a believable world that your readers can really imagine walking around in.

MAP MAKING

One of my favourite parts of worldbuilding is making the map. You don't need to be an amazing artist; a child-like scrawl on the back of an envelope is good enough, as long as it makes sense to you so that you don't end up getting lost in your own world. Which, believe me, is surprisingly easy.

Imagine your characters are travelling from A to B. If, in one chapter, B lies west of A, and then, suddenly, it's south, your readers will notice. Or if B is a coastal town one minute, and a village in the mountains the next, your readers will notice, and it will drag them out of your story. Plus, they will love to call you up on it. They'll email you. They'll message you on social media. And they'll write it in their reviews.

As an author, your job is to keep them in the story. To keep them believing that it's real. To blur out their real world, their real life, and construct a new one for them, for as long as they're reading your book. Glaring inaccuracies will pluck them out of your world. Inaccuracies break the illusion, and remind them that they are simply reading a story. That they're not a hero fighting against a terrible foe. It pulls them back to their own cold, harsh, boring reality. And no one wants that!

And so, at the writing stage, your world map is for you. If you're not confident in your artistic abilities, there are plenty of artists who can create a stunning map to go into the front of your book. At this stage, the map is only for your eyes. Build it out of Lego, build it on Minecraft, mould it from clay, or cake, or whatever. As long as it's useful to you (and you're not tempted to eat it!)

And don't be tempted to simply draw a map and then randomly scatter towns across it. That doesn't happen, it's not believable. Towns are founded in specific places for specific reasons. The main reason being, of course, survival.

So, imagine you're choosing a place to establish a town. What do you need? What considerations do you need to make?

Fresh water source:
The most important and first consideration. Have you ever noticed how many major cities have a river flowing through them?

Varied food source:
Man cannot live by bread alone. Or cake, sadly. Their food source needs to be varied enough to keep them healthy.

Natural resources:
They need enough resources to be able to build their homes, and the things they need. They can also use these resources for trade.

Appropriate land for crops/animals:
The landscape they choose to settle in will hugely impact the kind of food and animals they farm.

Access and security:
Can they get in and out of their settlement easily while still keeping it protected from intruders?

Trade route:
Can traders visit their settlement? Is it on a major trade route, or will they have to rely on people making a special trip?

Predators:
What lives in the woods? Or the mountains? How do they protect themselves against it?

People, by and large, will choose the easiest option for their home, unless the benefits outweigh the dangers or struggles. For example, you might consider it foolish to establish a town in the middle of a dragon breeding ground. But what if just one dragon scale (which could be naturally shed) would sell for a price that could feed a family for three months. Then, it may well be worth it.

NAMING PLACES

There are several different ways to name the places on your map. Remember that it's not just towns and cities you need to name. Depending on how big your map is, you might be naming mountain ranges, rivers, forests, counties, countries, oceans, continents, or even planets.

Just like places on your map aren't randomly placed, neither are they randomly named. They might be named after their founder, or the landscape, or the natural resources, the wildlife, the river or mountain they're close to. They might be named after a local legend; your place names can actually conjure up stories of their own.

Of course, you can backward engineer these things. You can find the name for a place, and then create the reason it was named that. Perhaps no one remembers. Perhaps it doesn't matter to you, or your characters, or your story. As I'll discuss in the next section, you don't need a full and complete history for everything.

There are so many online naming generators. Simply do a search, and you'll find countless. I have two that I favour:

- squid.org/rpg-random-generator
- seventhsanctum.com

HISTORY

Your current world is a product of everything that ever happened there, even if no one in your world still remembers. It's your job, as the writer, to know. To remember what they can't.

I'm not saying that you need to plot out 5 million years' worth of history. Unless you're into that. Some people are. But you definitely need to know enough to understand why things are the way they are. To know enough to effectively create the world, its culture, and values.

As people, we act according to our culture. And each culture is different. And there are variations in that culture. The things we value. The things we see as rude, or polite, or unnecessary. The things we want, the things we avoid. Religion. Festivals. The way we treat our elderly. The way we treat children. The kind of food we eat, and the way in which we eat it. The kind of jobs we do. The differences between rich and poor. The differences between high culture and low culture.

And these things change over time. Invading cultures. Migrating cultures. Important events. A war, or a natural disaster can hugely change a place's culture. Changing what's important to them. Changing the way they live their lives.

And you need to remember that every time something changes, it affects everything else.

There are different levels at which an event can occur.

International events:
Something that affects the entire world. Like climate change, population explosion, the sun dying, zombie apocalypse, etc

National events:
Something that affects the country or large area. Like an economic crash, natural disasters, death of a monarch, etc.

Local events:
Something that affects a town or community. Harvest failure, flood, local elections, introduction of a new predator, a new trade deal, etc.

Individual events:
Something that affects one person or family. Bereavement, loss of employment, loss of home, births, marriages, a lottery win, etc.

It's obvious how an international event affects everything else. I'm sure a worldwide zombie outbreak would affect you and your family. But what about the other way round?

So, imagine a family preparing for a wedding. They order a whole load of wine from the next village. That gives the farmer enough money to finally live out his dream of buying a boat and exploring the seas. When the winter rains come, the lack of the vineyard on the hillside causes a landslip which demolishes the mining town below, which leads to a shortage of minerals, which leads to a shortage of coins, which results in an economic crash.

This is, of course, a somewhat extreme example, but it's an important thing to bear in mind. Think about the butterfly effect, and the ripples you might be sending out.

Imagine your world as a pool. Every event, ever construct, every thing you change or create, is like dropping a pebble into the water. Sometimes, the ripples last a few minutes. Sometimes, a few years. Spreading wider. Affecting more people. Sometimes, those ripples last for centuries.

HOW YOUR WORLD AFFECTS CHARACTER AND STORY

You can also use your worldbuilding to create conflict. Remember that conflict is created when your protagonist's goal is interrupted, or opposed, and you can use your world to do that.

Perhaps the most obvious example is if the protagonist's goal requires them to break the law. But you can use other things too: limitations of magic, social norms and expectations, gender roles. The landscape itself can become a physical barrier, or the weather, or a lack of resources.

And you can use all of this in your worldbuilding to raise the stakes. To increase the tension.

Because your world doesn't exist separately from the people who live in it, and you should create it with those people in mind. They will have opinions about everything. Beliefs, hopes, grievances. Things they love, things they hate. Things they want to change. Things they fight to change.

And these things will differ based on all of their nuances: gender, age, class, religion, etc. So their opinions will be different to the person stood next to them. They may even directly oppose one another. Conflict.

You have to remember that everything comes back to character. You have to remember that you aren't writing a story about a world that happens to have people living in it. You are writing a story about people who happen to live in a particular world.

Worldbuilding. Story. Character. None of these is independent from the others.

CREATING A TIMELINE

Creating a timeline for the history of your world seems like a daunting task, right? Of course it does. You're imagining the historical timelines you studied at school: the industrial revolution, the dark ages, thc pyramids, ancient Rome, cavemen. All the way back to tyrannosaurus rex. Of course that's a scary thought.

But, don't panic, worldbuilder, because I'm going to let you in on a little secret. Check over your shoulder quickly, make sure no one's in earshot. Are we alone? Good. Here's the thing: you do not need to map out millions of years worth of history. Let me say that again: you don't need millions of years of history. You really don't. Heck, I can't even remember what I did last Tuesday.

On the following pages, I want you to create a timeline of all the important moments in your world's history. Important moments, not every moment. Things that changed it, either physically, or ideologically.

This might be a natural disaster that caused a splitting of an entire country, or raised mountains out of the sea. Maybe it reduced landmass, threw the world into an ice age, or sent the planet floating off into space. Things that really had an impact. Things that would have been noticed, right? Don't write down the year that average rainfall increased by 2mm. Don't write down the year 5 people died in a minor landslip. Unless, of course, those people were the monarch and family which caused a 10-year civil war.

Think about the big changes in society, too. The year that the first election was held, or the last. The year a king came to succession and promptly outlawed chocolate. That would definitely change a society. Or the years in which the birthrate halved, and then stopped altogether. The five-year war, and the following five-year famine, and the following eradication of inequality (we can hope, right?) The election of a dystopian government, the introduction of ID implants, the day that 10 million of them simultaneously exploded inside their hosts.

Big changes. The big ripples. The ones that lasted for years and years. Maybe they're still going.

BUT, I don't want you to do this right now. If you already have an event in mind; an apocalyptic event, a coronation, a special birth, something that changed the course of history, you can absolutely put that in. Sometimes, that moment is the thing that sparked off a story idea in the first place. If you have an event rattling around in your brain, write it down. Don't lose it.

As for the rest of the timeline, leave it blank for now. Use this timeline as a living document. Work your way through the rest of the book, and keep turning back to add more. You don't need to know everything up front. You can even cross things out, move them, change them, dump them. Histories aren't made in a day.

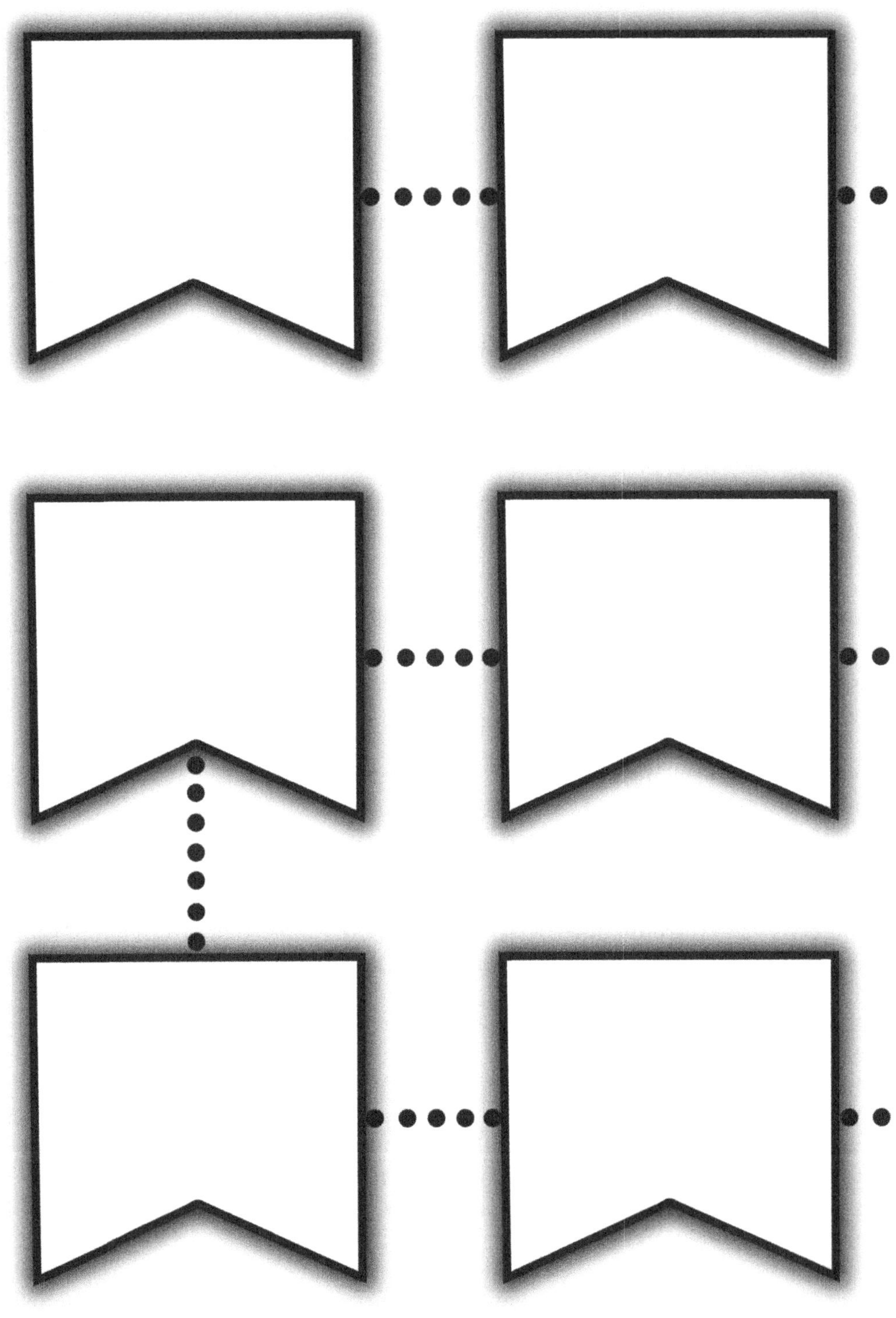

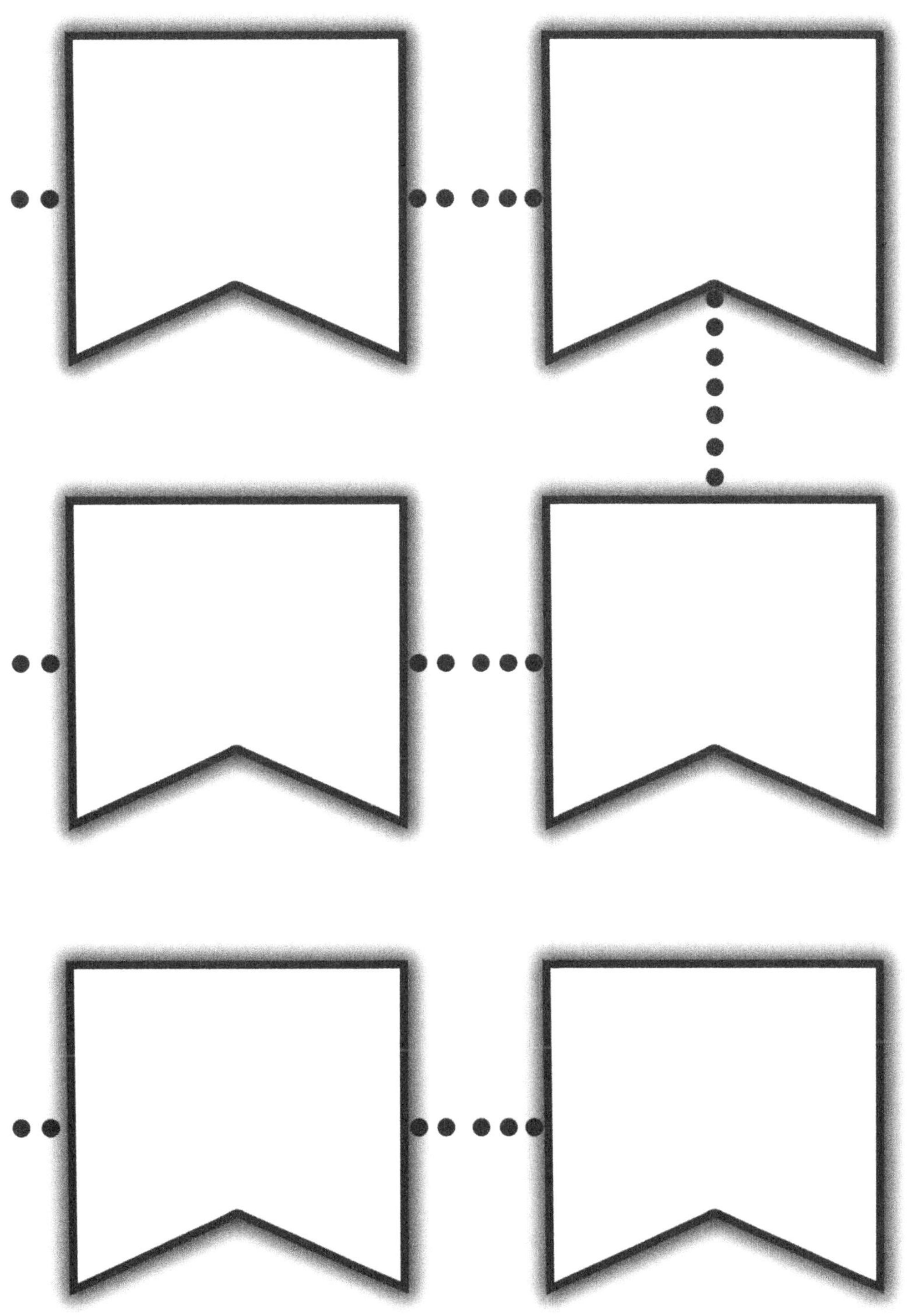

MAKING YOUR HISTORY WORK HARD

If you've ever written a short story, or a piece of flash fiction, you'll know all about word economy. When you have a tight wordcount limit in which to tell your story, along with developing believable characters, and creating a setting for them, and exploring themes, giving a satisfying ending, and so on, you'll know all about picking words that work hard for you.

Worldbuilding is no different. Just like when you're editing prose, you want to cut out any superfluous bits. Any bits that aren't serving the story. If your character describes a historic event to a friend, for no reason other than to fill that page, cut it. It's not serving your story or your readers.

If, however, that historic event has an impact on your character, the plot, or the setting, then it matters. Every part of your worldbuilding needs to be working hard for you, by either developing your character, pushing the plot forwards, or exploring the themes of your novel.

When you're creating your history, and filling in your timeline with significant events, think carefully about how they impact the present: the time in which your story actually happens. Think carefully about how they impact your character, and interrupt, assist, or derail their pursuit of their goal. Think carefully about how a historic event can become an inciting incident, that actually sends your character on their journey.

History might affect your character and their journey directly: they might need to find a long-lost artefact, they might uncover a long-forgotten magical ability, an ancient text might forbid them from their desires. Or it might affect your character via your worldbuilding: through long-held prejudices or superstitions, through ingrained gender roles and expectations, or through an ancient, secret society that has been feeding lies to a community for centuries.

I'll return, again, to my analogy with pools and pebbles. Every historical event is like a pebble that's been dropped into the water. Some are large, some are smaller, some are little more than grains of sand. Adrift, in the centre of the pool, is your main character, in a paper boat. The historical events you're concerned with are the ones with ripples that rock that boat. From the ones that gently bob it, to those that threaten to capsize it completely.

Whatever history you're including in your book, make sure it is still relevant in the present. Relevant to your story, to your world, and, most of all, to your characters.

Use the following pages to brainstorm how events from your timeline might impact your character's life; their life when the story starts, their life as they journey towards their goal, and their life once they reach it. Make sure each of those events are working hard for you: pushing the plot forward, exploring themes, or revealing character.

EVENT:
DESCRIPTION:
ROLE IN STORY:

EVENT:
DESCRIPTION:
ROLE IN STORY:

EVENT:
DESCRIPTION:
ROLE IN STORY:

EVENT:
DESCRIPTION:
ROLE IN STORY:

EVENT:
DESCRIPTION:
ROLE IN STORY:

EVENT:
DESCRIPTION:
ROLE IN STORY:

EVENT:
DESCRIPTION:
ROLE IN STORY:

EVENT:
DESCRIPTION:
ROLE IN STORY:

EVENT:
DESCRIPTION:
ROLE IN STORY:

EVENT:
DESCRIPTION:
ROLE IN STORY:

EVENT:
DESCRIPTION:
ROLE IN STORY:

EVENT:
DESCRIPTION:
ROLE IN STORY:

SOCIETAL IMPACT

First up, we're going to look at ways in which historical events may have impacted the society of your world. For the sake of this chapter, I'm talking about the people themselves. In the next chapter we'll look at the impact on institutions.

There are many ways in which history might forge how society develops and progresses, moulding and shaping it. Historical events may have had a big impact, completely changing the way society interacts and the way it's organised. For example, a war or a pandemic that wipes out most of the male population might change a previously patriarchal society to a matriarchal one. Or the discovery of a new energy source might entirely change the things that a society values. A natural disaster might cut off a community for centuries, leaving them to evolve and develop in an entirely different way to the rest of the world.

On the other hand, the impact of historical events might be more subtle, harder to notice, or confined to particular isolated pockets of society. An event may have rooted a prejudice into a certain community, or into a certain demographic. A deeply-seeded mistrust or dislike of another group of people. It may cause people to view certain others in a certain way: as evil, as stupid, as gullible, vicious, murderous, cruel, etc. And, as I'm sure you'll know; reputations are far harder to get rid of than they are to acquire.

Perhaps a historic event gave rise to a superstition. Maybe the older generation have good luck rituals, or particular flowers that they never allow inside the house, or a curse they mutter upon hearing the call of a certain bird. Perhaps the superstition is dying out. Perhaps people are ridiculed for still continuing it. Or, maybe, it has gained strength, or gained new meaning, or been validated by a second event in the more recent past.

Historic events may have changed the norms and values of a society. Increased scarcity of an object can certainly make it more valuable, likewise an increased supply of something often lowers its value. But, more abstract things will go up and down in importance and value, whether in the consciousness of an entire society, or an individual. Things like companionship, or time alone. Family, freedom, fresh air, good health and exercise. The importance of such things wax and wane through our lifetimes depending on what happens to and around us. The loss of a close friend or family member can change what we view as important, or a violent crime happening on our street. On a larger scale, an apocalyptic event can make water more expensive than diamonds, or turn once-crowded cities into places to avoid.

Gender roles can also change. Perhaps magic was only taught to boys until girls won a hard-fought revolution, or maybe a girl was born with more magical power than had been seen for centuries, leading to widespread testing of magical potential in all girls. Perhaps huge losses of the female population leads to them taking on a deity-like status, banned from doing any work or chores at all. Maybe genetic manipulation to increase fertility has left men with severely damaged lungs, and confined them to protectively sealed rooms. Maybe women have forged on as before. Maybe they've changed society beyond all recognition.

Historic events can also cause huge rifts in society, pitching one half against the other. A political segregation, a religious, cultural, or racial one, or an ideological one. Perhaps the arguments are settled peacefully, or democratically. Perhaps they cause violent protests or civil war. Maybe the rifts can, somehow, be mended. Maybe they cannot.

Society may become fragmented and split, with gaps between different demographics widening. Perhaps class divides become more prominent, with inequality increasing over the generations.

Alternatively, an event can bring society together. It can join communities, and heal age-old disagreements. It can remind people that their differences aren't so different after all. Or, at least, they can gain a mutual respect for one another, however grudging. Perhaps they discover that their only saviours from disaster are their oldest enemies. Perhaps they have to put arguments aside and work together for a greater cause.

When you're looking at the impact that events from the past have had on the present, you can work in either direction. You can create an event, and work from that, figuring out what changes it might set in motion. Remember; these changes might be instant, or they might be far more gradual. They may be easily adopted, and gratefully received, or they may be resisted, with people pushing back until they have no choice but to resign from their cause. And, how are such changes pushed through? Perhaps they happen naturally, with the collective conscience shifting over time. Perhaps they are forced through by changes in policy, in leadership, perhaps at gunpoint. Maybe change is inevitable and unavoidable. Forced in by something out of people's control, or, at least, something they have lost control of. A poisoning of the atmosphere, rising sea levels, the extinction of bees.

Alternatively, you can create your society, and work your way backwards. Rather than asking yourself "what if?" ask yourself "why?" Why has society become the way it is? What has caused this, or this, or this? Why would people start doing things this way, or feeling like this? Backwards engineer history until you see the dominoes that have fallen before.

On the following page, brainstorm the societal impact of your historic events. Working either backwards, or forwards, or, indeed, in both directions. And remember to always be thinking "how will this affect my character? How does it impact their pursuit of their goal? How can it create conflict?"

INSTITUTIONAL IMPACT

In the same way historical events have impacted society and its structure, they will have impacted your world's institutions too.

Events could have been the catalyst for a new institution being founded. Perhaps a charitable or non-profit organisation was created following a devastating war, or natural disaster, or widespread famine. Perhaps a change in the law created extensive poverty, or persecution, or homelessness. Or maybe enslaved people were freed, or borders opened to refugees, or huge numbers of imprisoned people pardoned, and institutions were required to feed them, home them, educate, and support them. Perhaps these events required the organisation of new communities, new schools, new hospitals, or even new councils and governments.

Perhaps events required changes in law or governance. Perhaps the death of a monarch without an heir required an interim council to take charge while family trees were studied to find the next in line. Perhaps a catastrophic failure or deep corruption of a government saw a country fall under control of the army, or the courts, or a band of rebels. Maybe a devastating, worldwide environmental crisis put democracy on the back-burner while the world's leaders fought to save their people. Maybe some of these temporary and emergency measures ended up becoming more permanent.

Serious events may require new laws; removing bureaucracy, or pushing through approvals. Laws offering new rights and equalities, or restricting freedoms. Maybe new leaders are crowned or sworn in without the due ceremony or process. Perhaps a traditional time of national grieving is postponed until a crisis has passed. Maybe a new ruling class take charge, or invaders topple the government, or riots are met by military firepower. In the face of a huge, world-changing event, things can get flipped upside-down quickly and irrevocably. The world may never be the same again.

Events can also eradicate institutions. Perhaps the world changes, and some organisations find themselves no longer needed. Perhaps a group fighting for equal rights, or for social change, achieves its goal and repurposes itself, or disbands altogether. Or, perhaps, they suffer a defeat they know they cannot return from. Maybe an institution is forced to close after disgrace and scandal, or its part in fuelling war, or exploiting people or resources. In the same way, governments can fall, ruling classes can collapse, entire empires can crumble. Who, or what, rises up to take their place? Is it for worse or better? And what happens if no one rises up?

Religions can also rise and fall. They can disappear, be forgotten, or disgraced. They can be replaced and pushed aside. They can swell or wither as trends and fashions change. They can become a footnote in history, or be forgotten altogether. They can be picked apart to create new belief structures, with their gods, lessons, and traditions living on in new forms. Gods can become demons, and devils can claim their halos.

Again, some of these changes may take generations or centuries, some of them may happen in an instant. Were your people prepared for change? Do they mourn losses of the past, or look forward to a brighter future? How have institutional changes impacted them, and how are they still impacting them? What conflict is caused?

Perhaps your character is the hero to free an oppressed nation of its dictator. Perhaps your character is the new ruler they needed. Or maybe they create a new government, and leave the country in their capable hands.

PHYSICAL IMPACT

Certain historical events can also have an impact on the physical landscape of your world, whether man-made or natural features are affected, whether by man-made or natural causes.

Obvious examples are natural disasters: a volcano eruption, an earthquake, even a bad storm can change the landscape forever. Towns can disappear. Forests, mountains. Cliffs can crumble into the sea, islands can be submerged. In the same way, mountains can rise up, islands can be created, wetlands turned into deserts, or landscapes claimed by water.

Mankind can also effect huge changes. Farming the land, cutting down trees, draining marshes, driving species to extinction, building huge cities and networks of roads. But it's not just the development of human life over time. Singular events can have a long-lasting impact too.

Wars can turn lush fields into a wasteland. Ecological disasters can poison the land or sea for centuries.

And it's not just the bad stuff, either. People can also plant forests. They can divert streams. They can build impressive, and beautiful monuments. They can leave behind a legacy to be admired. Something that future generations can learn from, and be inspired by.

The range of different physical reminders that history has left on your world is huge. It can be large scars in the landscape; obvious reminders that are impossible not to notice. Or it could be a single monument. It might be a town marked on old maps, but missing from more contemporary ones. It might be a road that leads to nowhere, or is shut off by a security fence. Maybe it's bullet marks in a wall, a plaque marking where the gallows once stood. It might be the name of a town, or a street, or a building.

But while the physical reminders are significant, so are the ones that aren't there. The ones that have been plastered over, or destroyed, or erased. The reminders that *aren't* there can be just as important.

Think about *why* a reminder might be removed or hidden. Who removed it? Was it taken away because it marked a shameful piece of history, or a painful one, best forgotten? Has it been removed to silence a demographic of people; to remove their history, their culture, and the things *they* want to remember?

Who wants to remember, and mark a piece of history, and who wants to forget it? Who denies it? Who refutes it? What sort of conflict does this cause?

Your world may also have markers from the past that no one understands the significance of. Perhaps they have been given a new significance. Perhaps they are simply a mystery. Perhaps they have attracted urban legends and folklore tales surrounding their importance. Maybe this was coincidental. Perhaps it was done on purpose.

PERSONAL IMPACT

We've already looked at the societal impact of historic events; the affect on society as a whole. Now, it's time to zoom in, and look at the personal impact these events have on your characters.

This is the most important part of linking the history of your world up to your story. If your characters aren't impacted by a part of history, then your readers don't need to know it. It becomes worldbuilding for worldbuilding's sake. It becomes filler. Padding. You want to fill your book with importance, not stuffing.

Of course, you can work out more of the history than you actually put in your final book. In fact, that's very likely to happen. That's alright. It doesn't mean that your work is wasted. You, as the author, benefits from having a deeper understanding of your world. And remember that your characters can be deeply impacted by parts of history, or they may just be indirectly affected. They might not even notice the impact it has on them.

For example, your character's only connection to a part of history might be being forced to sit through boring history lessons at school. Or, at least, that might be the only connection they see. Because those historical events, as we've explored, have also impacted the society they live in, the institutions that surround them, and the landscape of the world itself.

Perhaps they sit on a bridge that spans a chasm opened up by an earthquake centuries before. Maybe their friends dare them to explore the abandoned mines dug out by slaves hundreds of years ago. The connection may be little more than that.

But, let me take you back to those boring history lessons for a moment. Perhaps those history lessons are boring because your character can't relate to them. Because they only teach history from the point of view of the majority demographic. Or the oppressors. The invaders. Perhaps the history of your character's people is being eradicated. Perhaps its been outlawed.

Maybe the cultural emblems they insist on wearing sees them suffer a string of detentions. Maybe they're threatened with suspension or expulsion. Perhaps they gaze longingly at the magic lessons their peers have, while they themselves are banned from attending.

Perhaps they go home and practice their culture behind closed doors. In secret. In clandestine ceremonies and hushed festivals. Perhaps they gather in an illegal library of banned books, reading about their own history, and plotting ways to revive and celebrate it.

Or maybe those history lessons are pure propaganda. Designed to produce an obedient, unquestioning populace. Designed to cause division and mistrust. Teaching untruths that perpetuate prejudice and ignorance. Perhaps your character sees through the lies, and sets about to reveal the truth, once and for all.

HISTORICAL MEMORIALS

Memorials and Monuments come in all different shapes and sizes. From impressive obelisks and imposing statues, to a metal plaque or a hole in the ground. Some are built to last, others are only temporary.

When you're creating a memorial for your historic event, think carefully about what you want that memorial to convey. Does it stand for a moment of triumph, or a time of mourning? Should it inspire people, or remind them not to repeat past mistakes? It may not even be in keeping with the present stance; a relic of a past ideology.

Also, think about what happens at the memorial. Is it to stand in front of, bow your head, and remember? Is it designed to encourage play and interactivity? Does it seek to educate, or encourage meditation? Does it reflect the atmosphere of the event it memorialises, or does it counteract it? Perhaps it's been reclaimed: turning the site of something tragic or violent into a peaceful sanctuary for reflection.

A memorial can be a museum, a graveyard, a hospital wing named after an important person. It can be a stone circle, the ruins of a building, or a single brick incorporated into something new. It can be a mound of earth, or a pebble, or a dry river bed. The important thing is what it stands for. Its significance.

And memorials can be controversial. They can become the repeated victims of graffiti and damage. They can be stolen and lost. They can be defaced and toppled. They can be demolished and replaced, whether to eradicate them, change their meaning, or to protect them.

Always remember that there are two sides (at least) to every story, and a piece of history that is a thing of pride to some people, will arouse anger, or sadness, or fear in others. A memorial may also have different associations, and unintended ones. Perhaps a statue of a person who did a wonderful thing for mankind is controversial because they were also known for their prejudice and harmful views. Or associations with violent criminals. Or they supported an oppressive government.

A memorial may be something people barely notice. A carved paving stone, a half-buried pillar, a wooden monument that has rotted away. It may be something they don't realise the significance of. A fountain, a tree, a bench. It might memorialise an event everyone is aware of, signifying an important part of your world's history, or it might memorialise an unknown person, standing as a reminder of just one family's grief.

Think about the events and people you want to memorialise in your world. Think about what that memorial should portray. Most importantly, think about how your characters feel about it. Whether they actively avoid it, or feel drawn to it.

HISTORICAL BUILDINGS

Just like memorials, there is a huge range of historical buildings to place in your world. From domestic homesteads to cathedrals, temples, castles, and lighthouses.

You can basically split your historical buildings into two groups: those that are still in practical use, and those that are not. For the buildings that are still being used, day-to-day, they may still be used for their original purpose—courts, defensive buildings, town halls, religious buildings—or their use may have changed. An old courthouse may have become a trendy café, a town hall may have become a library, a church might now be an antique shop. And for the buildings that are no longer in use, they might be open purely for tourism. They may be nothing more than ruins.

The juxtaposition between new and old, and original and repurposed uses of a building, is a really nice way to show the historic progression of your world.

Perhaps historic buildings are revered and protected. Maybe they sit happily in the busy city that's built up around them, sandwiched between modern, glass-fronted office blocks. Perhaps the old town is a much-loved and lucrative area, drawing tourists to its winding streets and quaint cafés.

Or maybe they are respectfully integrated into newer buildings. Forming the corner of a modern shopping centre, or offering a stone archway to the entrance of a cutting-edge research hospital. The relationship between new and old might be a happy one.

On the other hand, historic buildings might be treated with disdain, and viewed as an inconvenient eyesore. Perhaps there is no protection for them at all, and developers are free to tear them down at will.

These buildings will also carry associations. Perhaps of an unhappy past, perhaps of a bright, proud history. There may be buildings that represent good things to one demographic, and unpleasant things to another.

Or the associations may only be important to one group of people. The government may think nothing of bulldozing a church of one religion to build something else in its place. Or tarmacking a sacred site for a car park. Or repurposing an old slave market into a trendy wine bar. The change in purpose might be deeply insulting, it might be absolute sacrilege.

The way in which your world's society thinks of and treats its historical buildings is important. It says a lot about their attitude to the past. To tradition. And to different demographics of society. The government might agree to the bulldozing of one historical building, while paying to have another restored. What message does this give to the people?

HISTORICAL ARTEFACTS AND TEXTS

Just as a historical building can come in any size, shape, or form, so too can historical artefacts and texts. From gigantic statues to tiny gemstones, or from huge, leather-bound tomes to single words on scraps of paper, the only limit is your imagination.

Artefacts can be decorative, or ceremonial, or practical. Its use may have become obsolete, or the true use might be a total mystery. Maybe the artefact is incomplete, and no longer of any use. Perhaps it has been renovated, restored, adapted, or repurposed.

It might be a symbolic representation of a long-lost item, a part, or a reproduction of it. Such as a wooden spoon to represent one that rotted away centuries before, or a scrap of cloth from a historical uniform.

A historical artefact might be symbolised by something far more modern: a holographic rendering of an object, or a set of lights showing where the posts of an ancient wooden henge once stood.

While the actual artefact itself could be anything you dream up, think about what the item represents. You can follow expectation (an ancient sword to represent an ancient battle), or you can circumvent it, using something less expected. Perhaps by using a flower to represent that same war. Sound familiar?

Also, think about the feelings that object arouses in people, or the feelings it is *intended* to arouse. Does it seek to revere and glorify the war, or does it seek to raise awareness of the folly and devastation of violence? And whose intended message is being portrayed? Is the artefact used as propaganda? As intimidation? Perhaps it is designed to push an agenda of division, by vilifying a particular demographic of people.

You can think about your historical texts in exactly the same ways. How was it originally transcribed or bound? Where is the original copy, if it even still exists?

An important thing to consider is translation. When the original text was written, who was able to read it? Who was responsible for transcribing or translating it? What checks have been made as to the honesty of that translation? It may be written in a dead language, or one that no one can understand. Perhaps the text is merely representative, with its true meaning lost to the ages.

And the big question, of course, is who wrote the original text? Whose words are they? And for what purpose?

Maybe the sentiments or rules of the text are still lived by closely, word-for-word. Perhaps people take from it what meaning they fancy; whatever suits their existing beliefs, thoughts, and prejudices. Maybe it is considered to be completely outdated and no longer relevant. Maybe it is simply studied as a document of the world as it was before, not as anything that influences the present.

But, of course, for any artefact or text to feature in your story, it must have some kind of impact and importance. Be it intentional and directly, or unintentional and indirectly. The discovery of such an object could prove something to be wrong, throwing society into confusion, or inciting violence and revolution. It might be proof of something that was mere speculation, or dismissed as lies. Or it could strengthen an argument, and prove something beyond doubt. Whether to the benefit of your characters, or to their detriment.

ERASED HISTORY

There are many voices that are left out of historical records and documentation. Either through omission, or purposeful erasure.

Histories can be stolen. Cultures can be stopped in their tracks. Entire civilisations can disappear from memory and documentation. They can be reduced to mythical speculation and fairy stories.

Be aware of who controls the history of your world. Who documents it? And how does their documentation serve *their* narrative, *their* purpose? Consider, also, *how* history is documented: written words, oral traditions, photographs, video. Who had access to such documentation methods, and who didn't?

Let's think about why certain histories might be erased or missing from documentation:

Omission:
Many voices simply don't have access or means to officially document their stories. Poorer communities, rural communities, oppressed and enslaved people. They may be uneducated, or not have access to a means of lasting documentation. They may simply be too busy struggling through life to even think about recording their stories for prosperity: when you're focusing on how you'll manage to feed your children tomorrow, keeping a diary might not seem that important.

People may be omitted from history because their stories are considered less important, or not note-worthy at all. Perhaps women are sidelined in the history books. Maybe non-magical people don't appear in them. Perhaps only the history of humankind, and not paranormal beings, is recorded.

Consider how documented history might be skewed by these omissions. Consider how documented history might be poorer for the loss.

Most importantly, consider how it impacts the ancestors of these cultures: the characters appearing in your story. How do they feel that their history isn't recorded? That it isn't taught in schools, or celebrated in the calendar. How are they trying to keep their culture alive? What are they willing to do to set the record straight?

Purposeful Erasure:
Someone controls history. Someone decides what goes onto the education curriculum. Someone decides which festivals become national holidays, and which aren't even a footnote on the calendar. These decisions have been made, whether through ignorance, arrogance, or maliciousness.

The ruling demographic of people may deem one history as less important than another. Or less trustworthy. Or, they may erase a history because it contradicts their narrative. Perhaps it paints them as the bad guys (I'll talk more about this in the next two chapters) and harms their reputation or the trust in their version of history.

Maybe they view a certain portion of history as dangerous. Perhaps it's divisive, or likely to cause a revolution. An uprising. Maybe it threatens to topple them from power. Such stories and cultural practices may even be outlawed. Perhaps they seek to erase magical history, or the history of a non-human species they have killed off, or that they want to portray as nothing more than dumb animals.

History may also be erased because they want to keep the knowledge for themselves. Maybe magical books are hoarded in private collections. Perhaps ancient maps showing the locations of treasure stashes are locked in safes. On the other hand, they might be protecting ancient burial grounds, or dragon breeding spots by keeping their locations secret.

Histories may be erased through simple ignorance or ego, with no purposeful malicious intent. If the ruling demographic isn't diverse, if it is a single race, gender, socio-economic group, they may not even realise they're ignoring the voices of the minority groups. They may simply believe that their narrative is the universal narrative, and be completely ignorant of the subcultures they're not a part of.

Whether purposefully or accidentally, *someone* is controlling history, and choosing which stories endure.

But what about those minority cultures? Have they been lost forever? Are they practised in small groups, or in secret? Are they ready to fight back and claim their place?

THERE ARE TWO SIDES TO EVERY STORY

History is never singular. For every viewpoint, there's a secondary viewpoint. For every argument, there's a counter-argument. Villains and aggressors see themselves as heroes. Side-characters are the protagonists of their own stories. For every single witness, there is a slightly different account. A slightly different understanding.

A victim might be viewed as innocent. They might be viewed as deserving of their treatment. They might be viewed as unlucky. Maybe things could have been different if they'd worked harder, or protected their property better, or not walked alone after dark, or simply kept their mouth shut. Or maybe if they'd spoken up sooner, they could have been the hero. Perhaps they were damned if they did, and damned if they didn't.

Likewise, an aggressor could be an invader. They could be an explorer or coloniser. They could be a liberator. Maybe they're being cruel to be kind, or choosing the lesser of two evils. Perhaps they're simply giving fair punishment, or protecting someone, or doing it for the greater good.

Every person or institution, every situation, every event can be viewed in multiple ways. One person's unnecessary rioting is another's last option. Their only way to be heard. One person's needless war is another's only route to freedom. One person's order is another's tyranny.

Look carefully at the events in your world's timeline, and the people who have led them, recorded them, and fallen by the wayside. Consider alternative perspectives, and how these discrepancies and conflicts bleed forward into the present.

What tensions still exist? What arguments are still being fought? Where is society divided, and how long have those divides been there? How long might they last?

Most importantly, think about how this causes conflict for your characters. How it ties into your story. What events it might incite, what resolutions might be reached. How can you raise the stakes and open up old wounds? How can you disrupt the status quo? And how are your characters involved in that?

TRUTH, LIES, AND PROPAGANDA

Going further than the idea of history being controlled by one group of people through the omission and erasure of alternative narratives, is the idea of history being created to purposefully serve that narrative. Lies being told. Truth twisted. All to serve one group of people.

From certain perspectives being pushed to the fore, to the truth being skewed, or flat-out lies being told, history is not always something you can rely on. It certainly can't be relied on to be neutral and unbiased. Because history is full of unreliable narrators.

Look back at the events on your world's timeline. What narrative has been pushed? And who has it been pushed by? Perhaps they're seeking to distance themselves from a shameful piece of history, to admonish themselves of responsibility. Maybe they do so by vilifying someone else, and painting themselves as the victims. Perhaps they vilify their victims, and paint themselves as liberators, as freedom fighters, or the bringers of civilisation and peace. Maybe people believe them. Maybe some people know the truth.

There is, of course, several points at which propaganda can come into play: before the event, during it, and after it.

Rulers can justify pushing through a new law, or a decision, or choose to go to war based on a false narrative they've pushed in order to gain support. They can continue to garner public support with propaganda throughout the event happening, and they can portray a viewpoint that serves their purposes after everything has finished.

Likewise, they can use propaganda to gain support for *not* acting. For not bringing down a dictator, or stepping in to stop a genocide, or for not tackling poverty in their own countries.

Think about how the lies and propaganda are promoted; the actual means of communication. To be effective, it needs to be done on a mass scale. It needs to be stated by a source that is believed to be trustworthy, unbiased, and authoritative. It needs to have a way to spread through the populace; to find its own propellant, to self-perpetuate, and breed into the psyche of the nation. Critics need to be swiftly discredited and silenced.

Depending on the level of technology in your world, such propaganda may spread quickly, or it may take longer. Maybe it's passed on orally, with songs and dramatic performances, or in stories and anecdotes told in taverns. Maybe it travels in letters, posters, flyers, and newspapers. Maybe via radio, television, or the internet. Perhaps it's some kind of technology we haven't even thought of yet: news delivered via swallowed pills, or palm touched to palm, or in simulated rain. Who knows?

What's important, though, is the effect it has. And how it impacts your story, your characters, and the world they are living in. Does it stupefy them, numb, or pacify them? Does it stop them from acting? Or does it incite them to uncover the truth? Does it set them on a journey to clear their name, or see them running for their life?

HOW MYTHS ARE MADE

A good myth is rooted in history. A great myth has just enough attachment to verifiable facts that it could actually be true.

We all know how stories go; they become exaggerated as each new teller adds their own spin, or seeks to make it more exciting, or muddles some of the details. The particulars get changed and forgotten, heroes become more heroic, monsters more monstrous, and the stories stray further and further into the realm of fantasy. But, when there are still enough facts attached, that myth is much more believable.

Myths can be of the legendary variety; historical, epic, swords-and-sorcery type stories. Or they can be more like urban legends; contemporary myths rooted in modern life. They can be inspirational, depicting characters to admire. Characters to aspire to be like. Or they can serve as warnings, keeping people from harm, or preventing them from illegal or immoral activities.

Whether you're creating historical myths or contemporary urban legends, they need to be deeply rooted in the psyche of your society. Why are these stories told? What power and influence do they still have? How are they relevant?

Myths might be used to bolster the reputation of a community. It might tell of how they rescued the land they invaded, and claimed it from savages, turning it into a haven of civilisation and enlightenment. The myths might talk of their God-given right to take the land. Of how they were rewarded with bountiful harvests in soil that was previously barren.

They might be used to disparage another community. Tales of cannibalism and depravity, of cheating and fighting dirty. They might talk of how an opposing army came as snakes, rising up into soldiers. They might tell of how they attacked from the mountains, but were swallowed up by a volcano that erupted at the word of the king. Perhaps the nearby mountains have human-like rock formations, giving a sense of credence to the myth.

Myths may be used to keep people away from danger: trolls in the caves, wolf-people in the forest, sea monsters beyond the horizon. They might be used to discourage certain behaviours: thieves turning to salt, fruit becoming poisonous if it was stolen, children carried away by the bog-witch if they play too close to the marshes. Or it might tell of disobedient wives turning to stone, or lying men sinking into the mud, or of fearsome dragons, slumbering, waiting to return if the city's greed gets out of control.

Myths can also be premonitions of disasters: if the deer leave the woodland, the town will perish in flame. If a statue is toppled, the crops will fail for ten years. If a male heir isn't born, no boys will be born for four generations.

Or, they can be more like good luck charms, and tell of ways to prevent disaster: as long as a flag is flown in the town square, the river will never run dry. As long as the grave of a saint is tended to, the town will enjoy prosperity. As long as the market remains in its original location, the gold mine will always produce riches.

These kind of ideas are brought into the contemporary world with urban legends. Urban legends tend to be more focused on individuals; bad things happening to singular people, or a small group of people, rather than befalling towns, cities, or whole countries. But they still use warnings in the same way. Maybe they are modern re-tellings of older myths, adapted to revitalise their relevance and impact on people. They are often used to keep check on morality, commonly including bad things happening to amorous couples in secluded spots, or overly curious children going somewhere they shouldn't. Using a lot of the horror tropes, urban legends like to exact their revenge on liars, cheat, thieves, trespassers, and the promiscuous.

HISTORICAL CONNECTION

Let's start off by delving into the past, and looking at historical myths. In fact, with these myths, you can go right back to the dawn of time, writing myths about the creation of the world itself.

And, of course, you can have several different versions of a myth. Different variations of it. Perhaps one is far more believable than another. Perhaps one is more heroic and exciting. Perhaps one is more terrifying, and the stories have been watered down for children. It might be that myths directly oppose one another, telling the same story from two very different perspectives. Heroes becoming villains and victories becoming defeats.

Have a look at your world's timeline, at which events might have mythological stories attached to them. Look for stories that would be retold and retold over again. Timeless stories, even if the details change over the generations, the base messages would remain the same. So, think about story themes that are always popular: love, betrayal, heroism, death.

Look, also, for verifiable facts. The names of people who really existed in your world. Battles that really were fought. Place names, buildings, traditions. Anything that really happened in your world's past. And then look for links to the present. Perhaps statues and monuments still stand for the people mentioned in the myth. Perhaps there are streets, or squares, or scholarships named after them. Maybe their graves can be visited, or a plaque marks the house they grew up in. Buildings may still stand, or their ruins might be open to the public.

Pepper enough facts into your myths, and they will endure through the centuries, with a repeated arousal of interest as various people try to verify or expose them. Tie those myths to modern reminders, places people can visit, things they can still see, and you keep those myths relevant. They may only be of interest to the scholars and historians of your story, or they may be of interest to foolhardy teenagers chasing ghosts.

You can also tie myths to the landscape of your world. Perhaps that odd, flat-topped mountain was squashed by a giant. Maybe that split through the forest was created by a raging dragon. Perhaps a bridge that has been closed for decades for being unsafe also has a story of a ghost who likes to push innocent travellers into the freezing waters below.

Myths can be used to explain things that people don't understand. Depending on your society, it might be things beyond their scientific understanding, like the rising and setting of the sun, or it might be something beyond their medical understanding, like cholera outbreaks. Myths might be used to explain the unusual, the bizarre, the paranormal. Myths might be used to pacify people and explain away something they might otherwise be fearful of. Or, they might be used to instil fear.

While your myths can be tied into your world's history, they certainly don't need to be confined to it. They can still be very relevant to your people, and we'll explore several different ways to make them so in the coming chapters.

Old, half-forgotten myths can be suddenly resurrected. They can come crashing back into every-day life. What if new evidence turns up? What if something is discovered that changes everything? Something that shifts the balance of power, and has the potential to bring society crumbling down?

MYTHS AND MESSAGES

Myths are often morality stories. The good guys, who are good in every way, do good things, and win the day. The bad guys, who are truly bad, and get everything they deserve. Whether at the hands of the hero, by sheer dumb luck, or by falling prey to a monster, curse, or other paranormal means. A simple duality of morality. Good versus bad. Simple, straight forward, and very clear.

But is the portrayal correct? Are the good guys really good? Such a black and white depiction leaves little room for interpretation, but it doesn't mean that the narrative is right. Or fair. And it's certainly not unbiased.

The myth's message may be useful in keeping a particular group in power, by portraying them as liberators and heroes, while painting their opposition as evil. The myth's message may help to perpetuate oppression, or to justify cruel, inhumane treatment of a particular group of people. It may help to dehumanise them, and dispel any empathy towards them.

The message may come across as aspirational, encouraging people to work hard, or to be obedient, or to accept their position in life because of a promise of future rewards. Such a message might help with productivity across the population, or maintaining social order, or with retaining the hierarchy of power. It might discourage revolution and the uprising of the masses. Such a message might pacify people and discourage change.

Because, when you're looking at the message your myth puts across, you must also look at who the messenger is, and how the message benefits them and their campaign.

Messages from older myths, which might fall out of favour and lose their popularity, can be adopted by urban legends, reiterating those messages to a new generation. The details may be different, but the overall meaning might remain the same: be good, and you'll be fine.

For example, imagine a traditional myth about two young people who fall in love against their parents' wishes and are turned into two stone pillars (perhaps two stone pillars that still stand, that people can actually visit). The moral of the myth is that children should obey their parents. Taking those stone pillars (remember: a great myth uses tangible truths), the old myth might transform into an urban legend of a young couple who sneak out at night to meet at the pillars. Maybe they meet their doom at the hands of a crazed killer. Maybe he encased them in the stones. Maybe, if you visit at midnight, you can hear them scratching at the rocks, trying to claw their way out.

The particulars of the story may have changed, but the message remains the same.

When you're creating myths, think about the message they portray. Think about who wants that message to continue to be given. Who benefits from it? Whose behaviour is controlled by it? Most importantly, how does it impact your characters and their journey?

EXPLOITING FEAR

It's said that humans are born with two innate fears: the fear of loud noises, and the fear of falling. All the others we pick up along the way.

We can pick up fears through first-hand experience, the experiences of others around us, or through stories. We can also be afraid of something simply because it is unfamiliar. Because we have no experience of it, don't know what might happen, or because it's like nothing we've ever seen before.

There are individual fears, and there are more cultural or societal ones, commonly shared by a larger community of people. For example, fear of the nearby forest or volcano is likely to be a fear shared by a whole community. Perhaps these fears are based in first-hand experience: the landslip that happened ten years ago, the flood last summer, or the increasing boldness of the wolf population.

They might be based in older experiences, such as an earthquake that happened a century ago. There might still be reminders, to keep the fear fresh: scars left in the landscape, or smaller tremors that happen regularly. Perhaps, even, increasingly. So, even though no one alive remembers the event itself, those reminders will make it feel very real and raw.

When a mythical story is told to keep us safe, and away from danger, they tap into our fears. A myth about a giant sea monster wouldn't hold sway in a mountain village. Likewise, a myth about mountain trolls stealing babies wouldn't concern a population living in an entirely flat country. The myths that endure in these places, will be the ones that tap into real fears. The ones that are rooted in the lives of those people.

There are, absolutely, universal fears. People can die anywhere in the world, children can be abducted from anywhere, and any community will suffer if their crops fail. But fears can be more immediate, more terrifying, much, much more personal, to certain populations.

Sure, an earthquake can happen anywhere. Or extreme weather. Or famine. But, for some communities, this is a much more real danger. If you're already living precariously, it takes far less to tip you ever the edge. A country that has only ever experienced one bad earthquake in the past two millennia are unlikely to be fearful of suffering another. A country with a very temperate climate will be less fearful of an extreme weather event wiping out their crops. The danger isn't imminent, it isn't close. So it holds very little power. But for those living on fault lines, or in tropical areas, or the edges of deserts, these fears are very real. And very powerful.

When you're creating myths for your world, look at what people are likely to be afraid of. What has happened in their town, or city, or country to back up their fears? What are the dangers they face in their lives? Consider how these dangers and fears differ to their neighbouring towns and countries. They may be similar, and the myths may have only been adapted a little to hold power in different places. You can have trolls in the forest for one town, and the same trolls might be in the mountain caves for the next town across.

These cultural nuances, these differences, really help to bring colour to the cultures in your world. They help to make distinctions between the different communities. And where there are differences, there is also a chance for conflict.

Think about the superstitions that have come from these fears. What do the people do to keep themselves safe? It might be something practical, such as burning torches in a ring around a village to dissuade the local bear population from coming too close. It might be something more symbolic, such as burning a candle in your window. It might be an act that is nothing more than a placebo, such as tapping your door frame sixteen times at sunset.

And consider who continues with these traditions. Perhaps the older generations still carry out the old rituals, even after the village has grown into a vast city and the bears are long-gone. Maybe they continue the tradition for no other reason than habit. Or, maybe, instead of keeping themselves safe from bears, the myth has changed and adapted. Perhaps the same traditions now keep them safe from a half-man, half-bear creature that stalks the city at night.

As ever, keep bringing it back to your characters. How do they feel about such superstitions? Have they abandoned them? Do they roll their eyes as family members continue to practice them? Perhaps they publicly decry them as stupid, while, privately, they are terrified of not carrying them out. What happens if they don't do it? What happens if, one night, they forget?

WINNERS AND LOSERS

As we've already explored, there are two sides to every story. There are different angles, different perspectives, and different biases. There are those painted as the good guys, and those painted as the villains.

Sometimes, it doesn't really matter. If the myth tells of ancient heroes fighting ancient foes, with little bearing on the present, then it doesn't really matter who's painted as what. But, if those villains are a race of people, an ethnicity, a populace that still exist, then having them painted as the villains definitely matters. Especially if they are an oppressed populace.

Prejudices can run deep in a society, almost as if it's become part of people's DNA. Superstitions, propaganda, generalisations, and stereotypes are perpetuated over and over through these kinds of stories. And through jokes, through 'harmless banter'. They're reinforced through media representations and through institutionalised oppression.

Create a stereotype that a group of people are dirty, oppress them into poverty, and the stereotype becomes almost self-fulfilling. People see them living in the slum parts of town, and believe the portrayal to be true. What is there to tell them otherwise? Worse still, why bother helping to raise them out of poverty if that's where they're happiest? Push the narrative strong enough, and the public will barely raise an eyebrow when you cut their welfare, or banish them, or kill them.

This can be done with any portion of society, and you'll see examples of this in the society you live in. Whether singled out by gender, age, belief, sexuality, physical ability, whatever characteristic they choose as a divider. It's the 'us' and 'them' idea. Turning the 'them' into something less than 'us'. Maybe, even, into something less than human.

And just as there are losers, there are winners too. For every person who is oppressed and kept down, there is someone holding them there. Someone benefiting from their cheap labour, or from their invisibility, or from the things they've stolen from them. And it is in the oppressor's interests—very, very much in their interests—to keep that oppression in place. To keep hold of the power. And when you already have the power, you have everything you need to keep hold of it. You can control the narrative, of the past, the present, and even the future.

This is a fantastic way to create conflict in your stories. Taking myths that have travelled through the generations. Myths that have that rooting in history, that are tied to those verifiable facts, myths that feel real and ingrained, and you can use them to create widespread conflict. Deep-rooted tensions. Tensions that really feel like they belong in your world, and that they've been there for longer than any of your characters have been alive.

But, of course, your characters are here now. And they're not happy. What are they going to do to change things?

HOW MYTHS AFFECT YOUR WORLD

There are many ways in which myths can affect the way in which your world functions, and I've already touched on some of them in previous chapters. But, let's look a little deeper.

Myths can affect the way in which your society functions. If they have a big impact on the culture in your world, then they will have an impact on the way in which people live their lives. Myths might create a sense of national pride, or shame. They might create topics people don't talk about, or topics they crack jokes about. They might give rise to traditions and habitual behaviours. They might be the catalyst for superstitions or tales of ancient curses.

Imagine an ancient myth which tells of a long-forgotten magical ability innate in a populace. While there would, undoubtedly, be many people who consider it as nothing more than a myth, with no basis in reality, others may well believe it. They might dedicate their lives to rediscovering magic, and returning it to the people. There might be organised expeditions, or university courses based on such a belief. There might be religious groups that pursue such ancient knowledge. Perhaps even political groups that campaign for a funded study into the existence of magic.

Maybe the people who believe in magic are laughed at, and seen as foolish or childish. But maybe they start to gain influence, and move into a position of power. Perhaps they finally find the proof they have been looking for.

A myth that vilifies a certain section of society might create deep divisions in your world. It might breed prejudice, mistrust, and hatred. It might cause violence between different demographics of people. Maybe those prejudices bleed into the institutions of your world. Maybe the education system perpetuates them. Perhaps the justice system is biased and unfair. Maybe the government has removed rights and freedoms from certain people because of these myths. Perhaps those people are enslaved, deported, or killed. Maybe the bias is almost subconscious. Perhaps it's entirely intentional.

These are ways than you can use myths to create conflict in your story. When they deeply affect the systems and culture of a society, then they deeply affect all of the people. Especially those on the losing side.

Look at the myths you've created so far, and think about how you can deeply weave them into the fabric of your world. Think about how they can create inequality, or build barriers. Think about who is on which side, and what the impact of their position is.

Perhaps nothing is ever going to change. Or perhaps everything is just about to...

HOW MYTHS AFFECT YOUR CHARACTERS

Now that you've looked at the way in which myths might affect your world, let's dig right down to the individual level and see what impact they might have on your characters.

Of course, when the myths are deeply ingrained in society, the effect they have on your characters is obvious. If the myths affect the culture and institutions your characters interact with, then, to one extent or another, they can't help but be impacted by them. Whether they're aware of it or not.

If they happen to be on the losing side of a myth, one of the people vilified by it, they will definitely feel its impact. What happens if they discover undeniable proof that the myth is a lie? That the hero is actually the villain. What can they do with this information? Do they have the power to wield it?

Perhaps they befriend someone on the losing side of that myth. And it allows them to look at the world anew, becoming aware of prejudice and inequality they hadn't seen before. Perhaps they uncover prejudice in themselves that they are suddenly forced to confront. Maybe they realise that, not only have they been benefiting from the bias, but they are one of the people who have been perpetuating it. Even if they hadn't been aware of it before. How might that change their life?

But what about the myths that aren't ingrained in society? Let's look at modern myths and urban legends. Although the themes of these urban legends, and even the story elements themselves, may well be borrowed from more historical sources, urban legends are specifically designed to catch the imagination of the present. They haven't had time to be absorbed into the local culture. They haven't had time to impact on institutions. They are of-the-moment. Flares of a match, soon extinguished.

It's important to remember how urban legends work. They are recycled. They're recycled from older stories, with the names, locations, and details changed to keep them relevant. Any specific urban legend doesn't tend to have much longevity, although variations of it will repeatedly gain notoriety. And the themes tend to remain similar: warnings that terrible events will befall those engaging in immoral or illegal behaviour. Be that sneaking out after dark, acting promiscuously, trespassing or breaking and entering, speaking ill of the dead, or whatever.

Of course, there are certain legends that endure. Passed down from generation to generation. Things like saying 'Bloody Mary' three times into a mirror at midnight. But these tend to be things that teenagers try out at sleepovers and parties. It's rarely in the consciousness of adults as anything more than a memory of their youth.

We've already talked about how myths hold greater power when they tap into the real fears of the populace. And younger people tend to be fearful of very different things than older people. There are few adults worried about their parents catching them sneaking back in after curfew. Or a police officer catching them getting romantic in the back seat of a car. There are certain fears that we grow out of. Or, at least, that we pretend to grow out of because, culturally, it becomes unacceptable. But, even as adults, we've all had the odd night when we're scared to look in the dark mirror above the bathroom sink. We just don't tell anyone.

And so, when you want a myth to affect your character, think about what scares them. What are they fearful of? How does this myth have immediacy in their life? It may be that their generation are deeply affected by a myth, and their parents can't understand it. They might brush it off and belittle your character's fear. Even if the myth isn't actually true, and the danger not actually real, it may be incredibly real for your character.

A myth might hit a bit too close to home for your character to ignore it. Maybe it tells of something they've already experienced. It might describe a creature they're sure they've already caught a glimpse of. It might be eerily similar to how their best friend died several years ago. Maybe it's a myth about the house they've just moved into. Maybe they had already discovered something left in the attic that suggests the myth might actually be true. Perhaps the myth suggests that the person destined to be harmed is someone your character loves. Their sibling. Their partner. Their child. Maybe they try to deny it, but they still have a niggling doubt.

KEEPING MYTHS ALIVE

Some myths only last a generation. Others are retold for centuries. What gives a myth longevity? How does it continue to be told over and over, even as the world around it changes?

One way a myth stays alive is by retaining its relevancy. This might be through universal themes that continue to 'speak' to each new generation. Strong stories of love, or tragedy, or heroism. Stories that keep capturing people's imagination. If people enjoy the stories, if they find something in them that is meaningful to their own lives, then they will continue to retell them. Perhaps they relate strongly to the characters. Perhaps they want to be like the hero. Maybe the message of the myth answers their questions and problems. This relevancy may exist on an individual level, or a wider, cultural one.

Another way myths can stay relevant is by adapting and changing. Being updated for each new generation. Even when the overall story stays the same, changing the details can make it feel more immediate and more relatable to each new audience. Modernising the names and situations, updating the technology and vernacular all helps to retain that relevancy.

The myths might be written down in books, perhaps simplified and softened to be told as children's stories. Perhaps they are taught in schools, or recited as part of religious or civil events. Maybe a country's national anthem is based on a myth. They might be turned into theatre, songs, movies, or TV shows. Perhaps they're shared on the internet, with urban legends immortalised in blogs and videos. Maybe the characters become cult icons, revered as much as reviled.

Think about how the myths in your world retain their relevancy. Consider how they stay relevant to your society as a whole, and how they relate to your characters as individuals. What in those stories make them matter? What makes them important?

And think about how your characters access these stories. Are they told by grandparents? Did they research them at the local library? Maybe these are stories told, in the dark, among their friends. Maybe they're whispered about at school, or passed around as emails and texts.

Perhaps your character is obsessed with these myths. Perhaps they dedicate time to tracking down the truth or debunking them. Maybe your character becomes a myth themselves, their story told over and over. Perhaps they're proud of the legacy. Or maybe they want to escape the infamy.

HOW MONSTERS ARE MADE

In almost every culture across our world, and in almost every time period throughout our history, there are stories of monsters. Folklore. Legends. Look at the monster stories that already exist around you. Look at monsters from other countries and cultures. Look at monsters throughout history. When you're creating your own monsters, it's useful to look at the ones that already exist in the canon of human existence, so that you can find patterns, and universalities. You're not looking to appropriate or copy these monsters, but you can draw inspiration from them.

There are things that scare huge numbers of people. Almost universal fears. You know what humans are like, because you are one. So, start there. What are you afraid of?

Just as myths work best when they have just enough credibility that they could be true, the same works for creating monsters. A string of possible victims, unexplained deaths, possible sightings, the odd footprint, grainy video, or hair caught on barbed wire. These little clues are what help to make the monster real, and keep it coming back.

Monsters are created for many reasons. They might be made to keep people safe. By creating a monster that lives in the woods, or the mountain caves, or in the deep river, you can keep people away from those potential dangers, by making them all the more terrifying.

They may be created to encourage good behaviour. Perhaps the monsters only catch those out after dark, or only come to steal naughty girls and boys, or focus their wrath on wives who nag.

Perhaps a monster is created to explain something unexplainable. A string of bizarre deaths, either of livestock or humans. A terrifying noise heard each night that seems to have no source. A monster might be blamed for a deadly landslip, or a crop failure, or any kind of bad luck at all.

Monsters might be used as scapegoats, as a means to shift the focus of blame. They might deflect suspicion from the true perpetrator of a crime. They might cover up for an incompetent or uncaring police force. They might be blamed for the existence of poverty, taking blame away from the ruling class and their systematic oppression of the poor.

Monsters, of course, may exist for no other reason than sheer entertainment. Designed, simply, to terrify. Because that's the thing about monsters; they very often don't have a motive themselves. It's people that bend them to their own purpose. But we'll look at that in the following chapters.

Now, I want you to think about why your world might need a monster. What purpose one might play in your story. Consider how it changes people's behaviour; what does it make them scared of doing? And think about how real the monster is in your world. Is it a mere fairy story? Are people expected to grow out of believing in it? Or is its trail of death and destruction very clear to see? Perhaps it's just as real as you or I.

HUMANOID AND NON-HUMANOID MONSTERS

Monsters come in two main categories: humanoid, and non-humanoid. Humanoid monsters have human-like form. They walk upright. They may even look like an ordinary person. They may actually *be* an ordinary person. Physiologically, at least. Otherwise, a monster may be non-human in form. It might look like an animal or creature we recognise, or it may look like nothing we've ever seen before.

Of course, you can also play with this distinction, with monsters that are half one thing and half another, or monsters that shift between forms.

Also, remember that monsters can be either sentient or incognisant. Your monster may be intelligent, able to plot and plan, able to outsmart their victims. They may be fully sapient, and able to communicate with them. On the other hand, they might be incognisant, able only to act on a drive of pure instinct; to eat, to breed, to survive. And —this is very important—the sentience of your monster does not have to relate to how humanoid it is. You can have a fully intelligent blob of goo, or a brainless creature that looks as human as you do.

Both humanoid and non-humanoid monsters can be terrifying. Humanoid monsters, including actual human monsters, are terrifying in their familiarity. Because they look human, we expect to see humanity in them: empathy, mercy, emotional intelligence, a sense of right and wrong. We want to attach these things to them. We seek to do it. But when we come across a human without these characteristics, without a sense of right and wrong, without guilt, without a recognisable set of values, it's terrifying. Because suddenly, something familiar to us, becomes very unfamiliar. And that is scary. That unexpected twist. That realisation that something we thought we could trust, turns out to be very untrustworthy.

We make sense of the world around us from our own viewpoint. We attribute our understanding of everything in the context of our own life: our culture, our knowledge, our experience. When we're faced with something that lies outside of that experience, something entirely unknown, that is a scary thing. Because we don't know how to react to it. We can't understand its motives or predict its behaviour. We don't know what it's going to do. Do we fight? Do we run? With no precedent set, we can't possibly know.

Whether we're faced with a monster that is like nothing we've ever seen before, or we're faced with a monster that doesn't act in the way we expect it to, in the way we want it to, we're left in the unknown. And that's a very vulnerable place to be.

It may well be that your monster is never seen, or never clearly seen. It may appear as a shadow, a blur, or nothing more than bloody footprints. You may wish to keep it in that unknown realm, and never allow your characters to know their enemy.

Or, you might wish to create a being for them to stare right into the eyes of. Does that creature look back with intelligence? Or does it look back with nothing more than instinctual hunger? Maybe that creature pretends to be something it's not. Maybe it's clever enough to appear as something harmless, maybe even something helpful. Perhaps it appears as a tame dog. Or a police officer. Or a child.

APPEARANCE, GENDER, AND SEXUALITY

Classically, monsters have a terrifying appearance. When you're creating a non-humanoid monster, whether it's made up of known animals, or it's a completely unfamiliar creature, you can go all out. You can have fun and go wild. You might want to make it huge and furry, saliva dripping from its jaws, it's long claws scraping and scratching. You might want to make it skeletal, arachnid, with limbs that crack and creak.

When it comes to humanoid monsters, there's a few things to think about. All too often, monstrous people have been portrayed as large, ugly, deformed. As the opposite of the established and accepted portrayal of beauty. It can be problematic. It can enforce stereotypes and prejudice. Of course, this might be a problem you want to highlight, and call attention to. But, before creating your human-like monster, just take a moment to think about the unintentional message you might be portraying.

Likewise, when you gender your monsters, just be mindful of how you're portraying them. So often we see female monsters as clearly sexualised (even if they're not portrayed as sexy), with breasts and sexual organs. We don't always see the similar sexualisation of male monsters.

Monsters are monsters because of their power. Because they have power over humans. Be this physical strength, or cunning, or an irresistible allure. You're free, of course, to create an obviously female monster, making her traditionally hideous-looking, and make her monstrous by virtue of her sexual desires. But just be aware of the message this gives. Be aware of how readers will understand your intentions.

But we do also recognise a different kind of monster. A genteel, attractive, desirable monster. Monsters that are sexy because of their deadliness. Because of the danger they pose. It's hardly a new idea, danger has always been alluring, because it's exciting. And there are sirens and sexual monsters peppered throughout folklore, their victims trapped through temptation.

It may be that your monster is never seen 'on-screen', so to speak. I suspect we've all watched horror movies where the monster lost its fear-factor as soon as it was seen. Because we're all scared of different things, and so we imagine monsters in different ways. Something that looks terrifying to one person, might look comical to another. Sometimes, it's best to leave it up to your reader's imagination. Sometimes, you might want your reader to come nose-to-nose with your monster.

Alternatively, your monster might not have any form at all. It might be a vapour, a mist, a shadow. It might change form. It might disguise itself as a normal human. It might take on the identity of your main character. It might simply 'borrow' their body for a while.

When you're creating the look of your monster, think about how it fits into your story.

In fact, you might want to hold off deciding what your monster will look like until you've figured out its role in your world, so feel free to work your way through the following prompts before returning to this one. Or, you might have a great idea for a monster, and want to build your world around it. There's no right way. You can work in either direction. Just make sure the appearance of your monster fits its role in your story, and is something that will be monstrous to the people of your world.

HISTORICAL CONNECTION

We've already looked at ways in which myths can tie into the history of your world, and you can do exactly the same with monsters. By integrating them with the past, you can make them feel organic; like they truly belong in your world. Like they've always been there, perhaps they're as old as the world itself. And, if they were there long before humans evolved, they're likely to be there long after humans become extinct too.

It gives them a place in your world, a right to be there. And if they have a right to be there, if they feel like they're an integral part of the world itself, then they're going to be that much harder to get rid of.

There are several ways in which you can tie a monster into the history of your world. Perhaps they're as old as the hills, and saw the very creation of your world. Maybe they played a part in its creation, moulding humankind with their own hands, before spending the rest of eternity terrorising them.

It may be that a natural event gave rise to your monster. Perhaps they crawled out of the ground after a severe earthquake broke it open. Maybe they emerged from a volcano, or walked straight out of the sea. They may have been born of wind, or lightning, or rain. There may be markers, reminders, in the landscape, showing where the monster began its life. A tree blackened after a lightning strike. A crack up the side of a mountain. The ruins of a town swallowed by a tsunami. Physical reminders give your monsters a level of reality. It gives them a level of believability. Even if just a little. But that small amount will breed doubt. And doubt is very good at growing.

It may be that a man-made event gave rise to your monster. Maybe they dug too deep into the ground, maybe they awoke something in the mountains, maybe they drained the wrong lake or felled the wrong trees. Perhaps they did something more ideological than physical. They forgot an ancient promise to the gods. They became too greedy, too violent, too cruel. They forgot their humanity.

Perhaps your monster is a manifestation of emotion. Maybe it grew from a nation's sorrow after a bitter war. Perhaps it was exhaled in the last breath of a dying king. Maybe it was the realisation of revenge, or despair, or evil. Maybe it was formed from the blood of the innocent.

But the events and details you tie your monster to, the names and memorials, all serve to make it more real. And when it's more real, it's more terrifying. It has more influence. More power. And that's what making monsters is all about; the impact they have on your characters and your story. The conflict they cause. And the blood that they shed.

MONSTERS AND MESSAGES

Just like myths, monsters can be used to give people a message: to inspire them to act in a particular way, and to warn them off other behaviours. Of course, with monsters, it's not a second-hand, veiled threat, wrapped up in a story of something happening to other people. The repercussions are coming straight to your door. And they're coming with teeth and claws this time.

Monsters might be stories told to children to warn against bad behaviour. Maybe it's to keep them away from the woods, or the lake, or somewhere they might come to harm. Perhaps it encourages hard work, or enforces a strict bedtime.

Monsters might be attracted to particular emotions. Maybe anger attracts a monster to you, or jealousy, or cruelty. Perhaps it's drawn to people who are unsatisfied with their life, or maybe its shadow falls on those who are sad, or grieving beyond the legal grieving period. It might be called up for those who are too curious, or ask too many questions, or are too nosey.

Think about how monsters might be utilised to cause conflict in your story. They might be a physical barrier, existing in a space your character needs to safely pass through to reach their goal. Or vanquishing the monster might be a condition of them reaching that goal. A monster can also be more of a moral or ideological obstacle, representing a terrifying warning against doing the very thing your character needs to do. Maybe the monster kills people out after dark, or those that disobey their leaders. Perhaps the monster kills anyone who disturbs a sacred building or object, or anyone who seeks to disrupt the established system of hierarchy.

It might be that a monster is specifically sent after your character. It may have been ordered to hunt them down, or it may have been specifically created for that purpose.

If your monster is being wielded by a master, this adds a whole new level to them. Because this makes it personal. Just as myths can be utilised, manipulated, and used as propaganda, monsters can also be used as pawns. But for what purpose? Is the threat of a monster used to enforce a curfew? Maybe it encourages obedience. Perhaps it curbs immoral behaviour. It might be used to prevent uprisings, or to oppress a particular group of people. Perhaps it will go after those people directly, or maybe it attacks anyone trying to help them.

Your monster can be used to maintain power and control. But, always remember that monsters can be wild and unpredictable. Can its master control it? Perhaps the monster goes rogue, and gets out of control. Maybe the monster goes way beyond what its master intended, or even fights against their cause. Perhaps it even turns its wrath on its master. Does your monster have a mind of its own? An agenda of its own?

Of course, your monster may well be human. Humans have as much potential to be monstrous as any drooling, rasping, scratching creature under your bed. And what's more terrifying than the depraved things us humans are capable of doing to one another? There are just as many urban legends about mass-murderers and insane killers as there are about non-human monsters. Such stories tend to offer similar messages against illegal and immoral behaviour; in fact, all too often, you can escape death simply by remaining virtuous. Whatever that looks like in the culture of your world.

Think about the message your monster gives to your characters. What behaviour does it encourage, or discourage? And who does this message serve? Perhaps it maintains the status quo. Maybe it oppresses people. Who has attached this message to your monster, how do they perpetuate it, and how does it benefit them?

MONSTERS AS MIRRORS

You can also use your monsters as another tool for highlighting the themes of your story, or as a reflection of the plot or characters. You can hold your monster up as a mirror to your story, to strongly project something to your readers.

If, for example, a theme of your story is loneliness, you can have a monster that takes people and holds them hostage in an abandoned building. Alone. Hopeless. Or you can reflect your theme of loneliness in the monster itself, with a monster who lashes out because of their own crippling loneliness. You can make them a sympathetic character, and turn your character's impression of them on its head.

If a theme in your book is family, perhaps the monster takes one family member after another. Slowly depleting a household, until just one person is left. Again, you can turn this around, and show the monster taking people to create a family of its own, desperate to feel that connection, and enraged when it's not reciprocated.

Beyond being used to explore your themes, you can use your monster to reflect a character or a plot point.

If your society is a dystopian one, focusing heavily on the systematic oppression of the working class, you can reflect this through your monster. Perhaps your monster prays only on the poor, prowling the slums for its victims. Victims that have little choice but to be out after dark, trying to earn a living. Maybe the monster gorges itself, greedily killing far more than it can manage to eat.

Perhaps the head of this society presents themself as some kind of generous benefactor, marketing themself with images of them rolling up their sleeves and joining in with charitable events. Maybe they publicly encourage charity, kindness, and equality, while leading a society set up to keep the hierarchy status quo firmly in place. You can reflect this character in your monster, with subtle, telltale similarities. Little reflections of behaviour, mannerisms, spoken phrases. Perhaps you turn your monster into a sympathetic character to further highlight the inhumanity of the head of this society.

To effectively use your monster as a mirror, it's a good idea to err on the side of subtlety. You want to gently push your reader towards their own conclusions and connections, rather than bombard them with blatant replication. Don't bash them over the head with it, simply give them a nudge in the right direction.

EXPLOITING FEAR

The fear your monster arouses must be relevant to your characters and the world they inhabit. If you want them to be scared, it has to be something that's scary to them.

For example, a monster that inhabits a deep, uncrossable ravine, is unlikely to have much impact on the day-to-day lives of your characters. If they have no reason, and no means, to traverse the ravine, the monster will not cause them much trouble. If, however, that monster lives in the nearby forest, a forest they have to regularly pass through to reach the nearest market town, that monster is going to cause them many more problems. And, if people regularly go missing amongst the trees, it's going to be even more immediate. Perhaps your characters have to travel through the forest the day after someone went missing. Maybe they venture into the forest to debunk the story. Maybe they find it's true after all. Or maybe the truth is even worse.

Likewise, a monster that stalks the night isn't going to be too much of an issue to a community that enjoys long, bright days all year round. But it's going to be a big problem to a community approaching a long, dark winter.

Remember that ingrained fears can pass down through the generations. A population can still be scared of bears, long after they've felled the forests and pushed the bears back to the distant mountains. And a community once ravished by disease will be fearful of any contagious illness, even if it's entirely different. And a country that once suffered a devastating earthquake will be scared of any tiny tremor, always wondering if the next one will be the end of them. You can have a giant bear-like creature roaming the city streets, or a monster that brings a mysterious and deadly sickness, or a monster below the surface, biding its time until the earth cracks open and sets it free.

Monsters can also play on more abstract, ideological fears, rather than concrete ones. Fears of loneliness, of being trapped. Fears of pain, or poverty, or madness.

So have a think about the fears in your world. They may differ from place to place, or there may be over-arching fears that are similar across your world. Make your monster relevant, make it fearful to your characters, and relate that to your readers. What are the stakes? What might your character lose if they fall foul of this monster? What might happen to them, or to their loved ones, or if they can't reach their ultimate goal? How can your monster raise the stakes even more?

Whether your character physically comes face to face with a monster standing in their path, or whether the fear of a potential encounter with a monster holds them back, the fear needs to be relevant and pressing to them. It has to be enough to stop them in their tracks. It needs to be enough that your readers wonder if they'll be able to push through that fear. And it needs to test your character, so that they have the opportunity to grow as a person. To prove themselves. To prove that it's possible. Your character is perfectly positioned to become the hero you know they can be. But they have to be facing their greatest foe in order to rise.

THE FOOD CHAIN

People like to think of themselves as being at the top of the food chain. While we are absolutely aware that there are many animals that are capable of attacking and killing us, it's not an immediate, every-day risk for the majority. I never look over my shoulder to check for loose lions while I'm walking around in the UK. Besides, as I understand, humans aren't exactly an attractive delicacy. While we might be attacked by a creature we disturb or distress, we're not really at the top of their menu choices. There are far easier and tastier targets.

So, when you introduce a monster that feasts solely on humans, that puts us in a position we have little experience of. At least, some of us. There are plenty of members of the population who are quite used to feeling like they're second in the food chain. Perhaps that gives them an advantage, and a level of experience that the perceived majority group don't have. Maybe it gives them an edge.

Introduce a predator that is stronger, more deadly, and even more intelligent than us, and it's going to get uncomfortable. The human population is used to having the advantage, and it's scary when we don't. When we realise that we're not quite as invincible as we thought we were.

It's scary for any creature to face their own mortality, and in many of our cultures we distance ourselves from it. We sanitise it and dress it up, or we hide it away. Out of sight, and out of mind. It's easy to ignore, and easy to pretend that we're all destined to have a long life, slipping peacefully away in our sleep. As an author, you have the power to interrupt that. Go on, bask in that power for a moment. It's OK to enjoy it.

Your monster's job is to unsettle the accepted norms. To subvert the established order. Your monster needs to take something away from the people, it needs to steal one of their comforts. This might be to take away their sense of superiority. To simply sit above them in the food chain. To be elusive, and cunning. To be more than they are.

A monster can also attack them less directly. It can destroy their food chain. It can kill their livestock, devastate their crops, poison their drinking water. It can take their children, stealing the next generation. Stealing the future. By doing this, it completely subverts the established order, and our understanding that children have their lives ahead of them.

Your monster can remove people's sense of freedom; trapping them into their towns, forcing them to cower behind walls, or set a night-time curfew. It can remove their sense of safety, leaving them scared to enter the forest, or have them constantly looking over their shoulders.

A monster can even remove their sense of humanity. They may form vigilante groups, hunting down murder suspects, accusing them, and carrying out whatever justice they deem appropriate. Without trial. Even without proof. And when the killings continue?

They will have to face the truth of their mistake. How will they reconcile it? It's a sad fact that we've seen this happen the world over.

A monster can take everything from its victims, and turn the world on its head. How will your characters face this threat? How will they adapt to a situation so alien to them? They're coming face to face with their deepest fears, and they need to make a decision. What will they do to restore order, and reclaim their spot at the top of the food chain?

HOW MONSTERS AFFECT YOUR WORLD

If the monsters in your world are real, they will have a big affect on your world. If they're mythological, the fear that they arouse, and the superstitions surrounding them will have an affect on your world.

Let's look at real monsters first. Real, breathing, actually existing monsters. They might be huge, terrifying creatures. They might be shadows or spectres. They might be nothing more than human.

Despite being real, there may still be people in your world that don't believe in their existence. In fact, the majority of people might not believe in them, or even be aware of their existence. There may be only a few people who have ever encountered them. There may only be one person who has. Perhaps people who believe are laughed at. Perhaps it's considered childish. Perhaps they're considered to be insane, and are locked away in institutions.

If knowledge and belief in the monster is widespread, or even universal, the structure of the world is likely to be affected, in order to keep people safe. There may be a curfew, or no-go areas. It may be illegal to do things that might attract the monster, like leaving meat in your bins, or keeping animals, or going outside when you're bleeding. The towns and cities might be arranged in specific ways to discourage monsters: they may be built far away from the forests, or with a fortified perimeter wall. The houses might be on stilts, or smothered in tar, or highly reflective. There might be traps or early warning systems around the towns.

There might be specific institutions that have come about because of the monster. Special armed forces units, religious groups, medical centres, educational institutions.

If there are particular people with a higher risk of being attacked (children, women, a particular humanoid species, or a specific race, etc), maybe these people are forced to live on the edges of towns and cities, to keep the danger away from everyone else. Perhaps they are protected in the centre of cities, in walled communities, or in underground bunkers. They might be subjected to invasive research procedures, or they may be offered up as sacrifices.

Let's now consider mythological monsters. While belief in them might be widespread in your world, the lack of solid, undeniable proof is the difference between these creatures and actual existing ones. There may be blurry, grainy photos. There may be unexplained deaths and disappearances of either people or animals. The monster might be blamed for simple bad luck, or poor weather, or outbreaks of disease. For the devout and the superstitious, this 'proof' will be enough for them to feel validated. For others, it will be questionable, at best.

But a lack of infallible proof doesn't stop people from being scared. It doesn't stop people from feeling the coldness of that monster's shadow. And that fear will have an impact on your society. It might be in the form of little rituals and habits people perform to make themselves feel safe: hanging feathers in their window, tossing chicken bones out of the back door, not wearing blue on Tuesdays. Whatever the rituals are, they will permeate into the everyday lives of your population.

Maybe such superstitions cause conflict. Perhaps people purposefully circumvent or oppose them to highlight them as being foolish. Perhaps there are those who toss their chicken bones out of the front door, or string them up as wind chimes. Maybe some people wear head-to-toe blue every Tuesday. Maybe they even paint their faces.

There may be superstitions that have become so habitual that people barely even notice themselves carrying them out. Or they may be so important in your culture that special feather wreaths are manufactured on a huge scale, and they not only hang in the windows of domestic homes, but in the windows of schools, churches, shops, offices, and even government buildings.

You can also think about the language your monster inserts into your world. Perhaps your characters use phrases like "as ugly as a mine troll" or "as wild as a wolf-beast." They might have curse words, blessings, or small incantations specific to the monsters in your world. Maybe it's not just bed bugs that might bite their children at night.

The extent to which your monster affects your world, from scattered superstitions to deeply impacting the infrastructure, depends on the place your monster has in your story. The role it plays. If it is the main conflict your characters need to overcome, then you can weave it deep into your world. If it's a momentary barrier, it can have less of an impact. Of course, you can also subvert expectations here. You can allow a monster that your characters discover is either non-existent, or nothing to fear, to have a deep impact on your society. Or you can create a terrifying, deadly monster that society is barely even aware of.

It all depends on your story, and the role your monster plays in it. And, whether your monster actually exists or not, is entirely up to you to find out.

HOW MONSTERS AFFECT YOUR CHARACTERS

Probably, the best place to start is to ask yourself this: does my character believe in the monster? Whether or not the monster is real to them will have a massive bearing on how it affects them.

They might be entirely convinced of its reality. They might carry out all of the rituals to keep themselves safe. They might be involved in a religion based around the monster. Or they might join the hunting parties that seek to destroy all monsters. Perhaps they go rogue, and take the task upon themselves. Maybe they have a very personal score to settle with that monster.

Maybe they're surrounded by other believers. Or, maybe, they're an outlier in their belief. Perhaps they're teased for it, or maybe they keep their fear a secret. It might be that they are the only person in the world who is able to see the monster. That it is their own, personal demon. That it has come only for them, and they have no choice but to face it alone.

The monster may be central to your story. It might be the final hurdle your character has to overcome before reaching their goal. Their fight might be your book's climax. The monster may, in fact, be the actual goal itself. Perhaps your character seeks to destroy it, or debunk it.

However, the monster may play a smaller role. It might even help your character on their journey, rather than being a source of conflict. Maybe the monster does no more than to highlight differences between various people in your world. Maybe you use it to reveal more about your character. Perhaps its existence is a minor hurdle for your character to overcome.

What's important is that, if you write a monster into your book, you make sure that it actually serves a purpose. It has to add something to your story. Either by developing and exploring your themes, revealing something about your characters, or by pushing the plot forward. No one wants a flaccid monster that's not pulling its weight!

Of course, it could be that your character *is* the monster. Maybe they know that they are, perhaps they discover it along their journey. Maybe their journey turns them into the monster. Perhaps their ultimate goal is to redeem themselves from their monstrous past.

KILLING MONSTERS

Is your character ready to be a hero? Are they ready to destroy the monster?

There are lots of different ways to kill a monster, and if you've created an entirely new and unique one for your world, then that method can be anything you wish it to be. From decapitation with one specific, magical axe to chicken pox, it's up to you what will finally end the beast's reign of terror.

But the important thing is to foreshadow it. Don't write a deus ex machina—a 'god from the machine' moment. If, in the final battle, your character happens to reach out and grab a rock that turns out to be a piece of copper ore, and hits the monster with it and, lo and behold, copper is the monster's kryptonite, then you have a deus ex machina. It's a conclusion that is so convenient, so easy, and so out-of-the-blue that your readers will be rolling their eyes and tossing your book aside.

Instead, what you want to do, is make them shout "of course! *That's* why copper was important before!" Something as simple, as common as copper can, absolutely, be your monster's Achilles' heel. But it needs to turn up in the story before this point. Maybe your character's superstitious grandmother insists on having a strip of copper across her doorstep. Maybe she hoards copper pennies, or buries them in the ground around her house. Maybe she's often muttering "it's not just slugs you want to keep out", and no one ever really knew why. Maybe everyone thought she was just a little bit crazy.

And that same grandmother may have given your character a copper necklace, begging them to always wear it. Making them promise they would. Perhaps your character doesn't like that "ugly, old necklace", and gives it to their daughter instead, who is strangely fascinated by it. Maybe the monster is oddly repelled by the child, coming close to killing her, but loping off into the forest instead. And it's not until later that your character realises that the necklace was the thing that saved their child's life.

Or perhaps your character's middle name is Coper, an Old English form of the word copper. Maybe it's their actual name that makes them the only one able to defeat the monster.

It may not even be a physical item that kills your monster. Maybe it just needs to have its power removed. Maybe turning your back on it, denying its existence is enough to kill it. Perhaps it feeds on fear, and when people are no longer afraid of it, it withers and dies. And when a monster is nothing more than a fanciful myth, simply proving its non-existence is enough to kill it. To end its myth, and end the fear the stories provoked.

A common trope in horror, and one that you can make use of, or twist around to create something new from, is the trope of the supposed saviour being beaten by the monster. It's the police officers killed by the serial killer. It's the exorcist slaughtered by the demon. The priest chased from the house he came to bless. It's a trope that's been played out over and over, but it's still a powerful way to raise the stakes and increase the tension.

Another monster-killing trope to play with is when the least likely person steps up to kill the beast. The person no one expected, and had been dismissed as useless and unhelpful. It's an idea that you can use to elevate a side character, or to turn your whole storyline sideways. You can use it as your main character's journey as an unlikely hero.

And remember that tropes are different to clichés. Of course, tropes can become clichéd, but you should think of tropes as journey markers. As milestones. They are genre-specific reference points. They are things that genre fans look for, and rejoice in when they find them. We all have tropes that we hate, and tropes that make us groan, but for every trope someone dislikes, others love it. I have a full chapter on the differences between tropes and clichés in my worldbuilding guide *How to Destroy the World.*

But you can also play with tropes. You can find new ways to use them. Even when you use common tropes in your story, it is still *your* story. It's still unique. Because only you can write in the way that you write. In your voice. So, don't be afraid of using tropes, just put your own unique spin on them.

Of course, killing a monster isn't always the end of your story. In fact, the death of the monster could simply be the start of it. It could be the inciting incident. It may have even happened before the timeline of your book begins, with the ripples and fallout of the act still affecting your world and characters.

And the killing of the monster doesn't necessarily make everything right with the world. It could be that the monster was the only thing keeping the world alive. Or perhaps something even worse rises up to take its place. Or, with the monster gone, a community has no more reason to exist, or society falls into chaos, or a huge industry dies and causes a devastating recession. Killing the monster doesn't necessarily solve all the problems in your world. In fact, it could be just the beginning of them...

A WORD ON INFO DUMPING AND LEARNING CURVES

Once you have completed your worldbuilding, and you are ready to start writing your book, you need to consider how, and how much, of this information to include.

Don't think that you will be including every ounce of what you've worked on. You won't. You shouldn't. I know, I know, you worked hard on it, but it wasn't wasted, even if it never makes it into your book. It helped you to understand your world, so that you can write about it in an informed, attached, and immersive way. So that you can make it all the more real for your readers.

An 'info dump' is the term used for when a writer pours out information onto the page as if they are writing a history text book. It's dry, it's dull, and, more often than not, it's confusing.

I'm sure you will have heard the old adage 'show don't tell'. This means that you should be *showing* your readers your worldbuilding, through action and dialogue, not simply *telling* them via a historical lecture.

The absolute best way to teach your readers about your world, is through action. This might be your character clashing with police, or it may simply be them navigating the world.

Let me expand on that: if something in your world is absolutely normal, however far removed it is from our world, if you character treats it, and reacts to it, as if it is entirely regular and everyday, then you are teaching your readers about your world through action.

Say, for example, centaurs are a common sight in your world. If your character treats them with no surprise at all, talking to them as if they are another human, then your readers learn that centaurs and humans live alongside one another equally. Or, perhaps your character ridicules, or bullies the centaurs. Or they treat them with respect, or fear. This is what you are teaching your readers about what is the norm in your world. Through action. This is the ideal way to show your worldbuilding.

It's not always so easy.

And so, the next best way is through dialogue. Again, avoid huge blocks of information. This is no different to info dumping, you're simply letting the history lecture come out of a character's mouth. However, they can have a conversation with a friend about a historical aspect of the world, or a cultural aspect. A conversation. Not a lecture.

Sometimes, however, you need to break the rules.

I'm not saying that you must never simply tell your readers information. Sometimes, it's necessary. Sometimes, it's even the better option. But, do it with careful consideration, and do it sparingly. Rules are, certainly in creative pursuits, meant to be broken.

If you're concerned about whether or not you're getting the balance right, the best way is through the use of beta readers. Beta readers read through early, pre-publication versions of books, and give honest feedback that allows the author to improve their story. If you've got the balance wrong, beta readers can tell you.

Another way to learn this is through reading, reading, and reading. Take careful note of how other authors handle the dilemma. How they get the balance right, and how they get it wrong.

The other way is simply through practice. The more you write, the more you drill down into your personal style and voice, the better you are likely to get at it.

The way in which you give worldbuilding information to your readers also depends on the complexity of your world, and how different it is to ours.

If you're writing about earth, whether in the present, past, or future, there are many things your readers will already know. They understand about time, and seasons. They know the animals, the plants. They know what humans are like, and how they interact. The learning curve of your world may be quite a gentle one.

Everything in your world that is different to our real world, adds to the learning curve of your book. Every mythical creature, every imagined technology, every drop of magic, and every jargon word makes that curve a little bit steeper.

You want to ease your readers in. If, in chapter one, you expect them to learn everything about your world and its history, learn who the characters are, and absorb their struggles and goals, they will be exhausted by the time they get to chapter two.

Tell them what they need to know. They don't need 5 million years worth of military history. They may need flashes of it, but not the entire thing. Be gentle with them. Don't make them do too much work, and don't leave them floundering around your story loaded down with too much knowledge.

Again, these are things that you can learn and improve on with the help of beta readers, by reading, reading, reading, and by simply practising your craft. You will find your way, I promise, but I can't tell you how to do it, because we are all different. And our stories are different. And our voices are different.

You might write short, 50,000 word novels, and leave a lot of the deeper worldbuilding out. You might write 130,000 word epics, with readers who expect a much more immersive experience. Practice, experiment, and you'll find the right balance for you, your books, and your readers.

IDEAS DUMP

As you work your way through this book, you are bound to have flashes of ideas popping into your mind. Character and story ideas, that don't quite belong with the workbook prompts.

Don't lose them; those little flashes are important.

Instead, use the following pages as something of an ideas dump. Some of these may never make it into your finished book, but, you never know, you may be able to recycle them into other stories.

No idea is ever wasted...

WANT EVEN MORE WORLDBUILDING?

Our adventures don't have to end here...

You can explore the rest of my series of worldbuilding guides for authors, guiding you through the basics of worldbuilding, helping you to create magic systems and religions, to write dystopian and post-apocalyptic fiction, and to create histories rich with myths and monsters.

Find more information on all of my workbooks and other worldbuilding services at angelinetrevena.co.uk/worldbuilding

Get Your Free Creating a Timeline Worksheet

Join my worldbuilding mailing list to claim your free Creating a Timeline worksheet.

You will also receive all the latest news on releases and workshops, as well as worldbuilding tips, tricks, and resources.

Join at subscribepage.com/worldbuilding

ABOUT ANGELINE TREVENA

Angeline Trevena was born and bred in a rural corner of Devon, but now lives among the breweries and canals of central England with her husband, their two sons, and a pair of black cats. She is a dystopian urban fantasy and post-apocalyptic author, a podcaster, and events manager.

In 2003 she graduated from Edge Hill University, Lancashire, with a BA Hons Degree in Drama and Writing. During this time she decided that her future lay in writing words rather than performing them.

Some years ago she worked at an antique auction house and religiously checked every wardrobe that came in to see if Narnia was in the back of it. She's still not given up looking for it.

Find out more at www.angelinetrevena.co.uk

Made in the USA
Monee, IL
13 July 2022

99615017R00057